I0816277

Praise for *Powerful Powders*

"An INCREDIBLY POWDER-FUL book. In the words of bestselling author Charity L. Bedell, 'Magic doesn't have to be hard. It can be simple.' And, after reading the book, I wholeheartedly agree. Not only was I mesmerized by her profound depth of knowledge in witchcraft and folklore, but Charity's sense and sensibility of working with everyday magical powders and spells helps aspiring witches to put her *Powerful Powders* to work for you. ...An enlightening, must-read book for everyone looking to elevate their magical practice. It's a treasure trove of magical insights and inspiration for all. Buy it now!"
—**SHAWN ROBBINS,** coauthor of *Wiccapedia* and *The Good Witch's Guide*

"Charity's fine book is both an introduction to powders and a guide for practitioners who are expanding their field of study. Well-written and chock-full of information, this book is a wonderful addition to any witch's or herbalist's library."
—**H. BYRON BALLARD,** author of *A Feral Church* and *Small Magics*

"Have you ever had a life moment after reading a book that made you realize that you found a classic in its first release? This is it. Whether you are a phenom in folk magic studies or just looking into a simple primer on the topic, this book belongs on your shelf. I even recommend asking your local library to add it to the reference collection. Why? Because it's that good. I should know. I am about this magical life and it's going on my shelf."

—KENYA COVIAK, folk magician/Hoodoo practitioner and owner of Detroit Conjure

"There's dust, and then there is dust. The first type is the dusty powder that's a household nuisance, but there are powders that are of the beneficial type as well. There are floor sweeps, edible magical powders, witch salts, and many more. Charity L. Bedell introduces readers to her latest book, *Powerful Powders*. It's one of a kind. Taught by way of exercises, recipe creations, and formulas, you will learn how to work with all of your magical workings. It's one of those books of wisdom that need to be in your bookcase."

—MARLA BROOKS, author and host of *Stirring the Cauldron* on the Para X Radio Network

"Ms. Bedell has crafted a book for beginning and seasoned magical practitioners alike. As she says in the opening chapter, powders are an easy way to create a tool for immediate use and also store that tool for quite a while. From easy-to-follow instructions for creating powders to suggestions for spells in which to use them, she walks you through crafting magical powders for virtually any need. This book should be on every witch's reference shelf!"

—DEBORAH J. MARTIN, MH, author of *Herbs: Medicinal, Magical, Marvelous!*

"*Powerful Powders* by Charity is both spiritually uplifting as well as magically grounding. There is so much peace, power, and connection when conversing with the natural world and the spirits of the land. Whether it is through the dirt in our gardens, or the powders of herbs and other substances; each of us can experience playful yet powerful magic. In this book, Charity walks us through magic and spellcasting ways to enhance our magical practices."
—**GRANDDAUGHTER CROW,** author of *The Wisdom of the Natural World*

"Charity Bedell's *Powerful Powders* honors her roots as an initiate of Conjure and a practitioner of folk magic while offering a deeply accessible pathway for any witch on their own journey to reach beyond black salt and begin working more deeply with powders. *Powerful Powders* is an empowering companion for any sacred wild soul."
—**ELYSE WELLES,** author of *Sacred Wild*

Powerful Powders

About the Author

© Photo provided by HMages: Photography by HM & Hilareigh Maxson

Charity L. Bedell (Maine), also known as Loona Wynd, is one of the coauthors of The Modern-Day Witch series and the Wiccapedia Spell Deck. She has studied Conjure with Starr Casas and Feri with Veedub, and she is initiated in the Temple Tradition. Bedell has written for *The Witches' Almanac* and *Kindred Spirit Magazine*, and she has presented at festivals such as WitchCon2020. Learn more at Mystic-Echoes.com.

To Write to the Author

If you wish to contact the author or would like more information about this book, please write to the author in care of Llewellyn Worldwide Ltd. and we will forward your request. Both the author and the publisher appreciate hearing from you and learning of your enjoyment of this book and how it has helped you. Llewellyn Worldwide Ltd. cannot guarantee that every letter written to the author can be answered, but all will be forwarded. Please write to:

Charity L. Bedell
℅ Llewellyn Worldwide
2143 Wooddale Drive
Woodbury, MN 55125-2989

Please enclose a self-addressed stamped envelope for reply, or $1.00 to cover costs. If outside the U.S.A., enclose an international postal reply coupon.

Many of Llewellyn's authors have websites with additional information and resources. For more information, please visit our website at https://www.llewellyn.com.

POWERFUL POWDERS

RECIPES & FORMULAS FOR MAGIC & SPELLCRAFT

CHARITY L. BEDELL

WOODBURY, MINNESOTA

First Edition
First Printing, 2026

Based on book design by Christine Ha
Book format by Samantha Peterson
Cover design by Shannon McKuhen

Library of Congress Cataloging-in-Publication Data (Pending)
ISBN: 978-0-7387-8056-6

Llewellyn Publications
A Division of Llewellyn Worldwide Ltd.
2143 Wooddale Drive
Woodbury, MN 55125-2989
www.llewellyn.com

Printed in the United States of America

GPSR Representation:
UPI-2M PLUS d.o.o., Medulićeva 20, 10000 Zagreb, Croatia,
matt.parsons@upi2mbooks.hr

Other Books by Charity L. Bedell

The Good Witch's Guide: A Modern-Day Wiccapedia of Magickal Ingredients and Spells
(cowritten with Shawn Robbins, Sterling Ethos, 2017)

The Good Witch's Perpetual Planner
(cowritten with Shawn Robbins, Sterling Ethos, 2019)

The Wiccapedia Spell Deck: A Compendium of 100 Spells & Rituals for the Modern-Day Witch
(cowritten with Leanna Greenaway and Shawn Robbins, Sterling Ethos, 2020)

The Modern-Day Witch 2023
Wheel of the Year 17-Month Planner
(cowritten with Shawn Robbins, Sterling Ethos, 2022)

Container Magic: Spellcraft Using Sachets, Bottles, Poppets & Jars
(Llewellyn, 2023)

Divine Dirt: The Art of Using Dirt in Magic, Ritual & Spellcraft
(Llewellyn, 2024)

Dedication

This book is dedicated to my mom, Linda Bedell. She has always been an influential force in my life. She taught me about tarot cards, angels, and spirits. She was also the one who bought me my first tarot deck. When it comes to my spirituality and magical practice, she has encouraged it from the start, taking some classes with me, and helping me find others. She was the first person to support my dreams of becoming an author and running my own metaphysical shop. Thank you for all the support, Mom. This book is my thank you to you.

Disclaimer

The publisher and author assume no liability for any injuries caused to the reader that may result from the reader's use of content contained in this publication and recommend common sense when contemplating the practices described in the work. In the following pages you will find recommendations for the use of certain essential oils, incense blends, and ritual items. If you are allergic to any items used in the exercises, please refrain from use. Essential oils are potent; use care when handling them. Always dilute essential oils before placing them on your skin, and make sure to do a patch test on your skin before use. There are spells in this text that deal with mental illness support. These spells are to supplement proper treatment for your mental health, and they are not substitutions for treatment by a professional. If you are in crisis, talk to a professional and get proper treatment first. Only use the spells after seeking professional help.

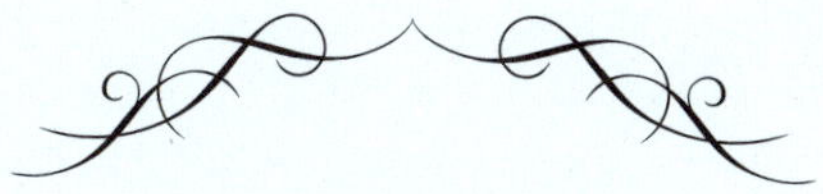

Contents

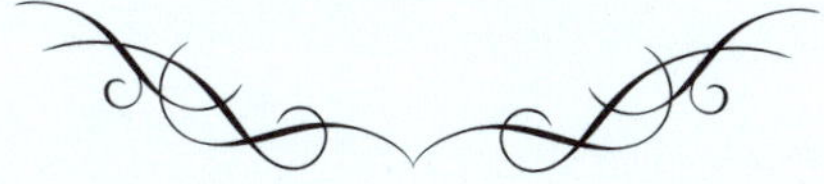

PART III: RESOURCES

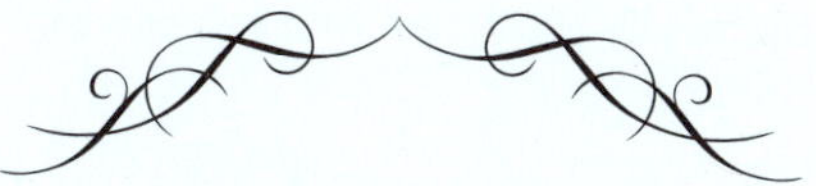

Introduction

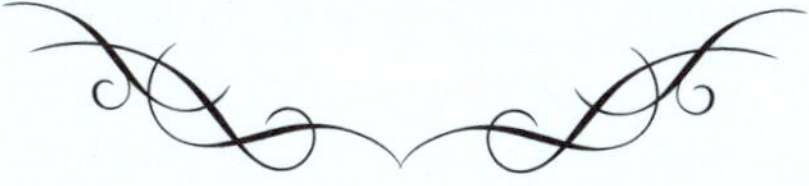

A young woman has just moved into a new home and needs to ward it. She takes a vial out of her purse and starts walking along the border of her property. While she walks, she begins to scatter the contents of the vial. As she sprinkles the mixture, she recites prayers, mantras, and chants to empower the protection. When she reaches the point where she started, she seals the vial once again and stands up straight knowing that her home now has a strong ward against evil and other forms of negativity.

A young mother sits with a small blue fabric dolly. She comes from a long line of cunning women and healers. In the room behind her, her small child rests, sick with a bad fever and illness. Tears of hope and love fill the mother's eyes as she fills the doll with a mixture of materials. As she does so, she whispers a healing prayer, calling on her ancestors. When the doll is full, she finishes sewing its head and sets it in front of a candle. Every day she lights the candle and recites the same prayers until the child begins to get better.

The two stories above involve the use of magical powders. Magical powders are powerful tools that can be used or adapted to any magical work you have in mind. In each of the stories, a magical powder provides the power for the spell being worked. These simple mixtures of herbs and curios provide all of the energy and power for the spells they were used in.

What Are Magical Powders?

Magical powders are blends of herbs and curios that have been ground to a fine consistency. These powders are often sprinkled or dusted over objects or locations to enact specific magical works. The practice of dusting objects and materials with powders is why some magical powders are referred to as dusting powders. Dusting is only one of many ways magical powders can be worked with, which is why I choose to simply call them magical powders rather than dusting powders.

The combination of various unique curios gives each powder a unique magical signature. Once created, a powder can store its magical charge until its power is needed.

The process of creating a magical powder gives you a tool that can be used instantly or stored for future use.

Why Use Powders?

Powders are versatile magical tools. They can be used by themselves as a spell, or they can be included with other materials for a larger and more powerful working. The creation of magical powders is an excellent example of how witchcraft is a craft. You craft the powders by combining herbs and curios, working physically and practically but also subtly and energetically.

Magical powders also give us ways that we can be a bit playful with our magic. As the energetic forces that make up the powder combine to create a cohesive whole, it is important to be able to play with the energy and feel how it meshes. It's a chance to experiment with herbs and other curios in new ways.

You can use powders as fillings for container spells, pouring them into poppets, sachets, jars, and balls. As a filling, these powders can be used by themselves or combined with other materials. As the powder is added to the vessel, a small bit of energy is released to start the spell process. The rest gets released a little at a time as the primary spellwork is performed.

Powders can also be used in spellwork by being dusted or scattered about the area you want the magic to impact.

Fast cash powders are often sprinkled in wallets to bring money into the household quickly. For candle spells, you can spread the powder around the base of the candle, or you can run the powder over the candle after anointing it with an oil.

About Me

I have been a practicing witch for twenty-five years now. My journey into witchcraft began when I was thirteen years old. I was gifted a copy of the book *Teen Witch* by Silver Ravenwolf. From then on, I knew that not only was I a witch but that my path in life involved teaching witchcraft in some way, shape, or form.

It was when I entered college that I decided I wanted to have some formal training. When I had a chance to receive formal training in the Temple of Witchcraft tradition, I took it. I was initiated to the second degree of the Temple Tradition in 2020. I also had a chance to study the Feri tradition in the Dustbunny line under Veedub, or Valerie Walker. While I have not been initiated into the Feri tradition, it has still been an influence in my magical and spiritual path.

The Feri tradition of witchcraft contains elements that come from Hoodoo or Conjure, and when I had an opportunity to study with a Conjure elder, I jumped at that chance as well and signed up with the Conjure Academy.

Today I am a proud graduate of the Conjure Academy and able to call myself a Conjure worker.

Practices Within This Text

The spells and workings in this book come from the basis of folk magic, and there are two systems of magic that make up the practices that are found in this text. The first system of magic is witchcraft. The second magical system is that of Hoodoo or Conjure.

Conjure is an American system of folk magic that developed during the times of slavery by those who were enslaved. They created Conjure as a way to preserve what practices they could from their homelands. Using brooms and herbal sweeps to bless and protect the home while reciting Bible verses is an example of how Conjure combined their ancestral practices with the Christianity forced upon them.

While Hoodoo or Conjure originated through slavery and persecution, the practice is open to everyone. As former enslaved people lived among other minority populations, the practice of Conjure began to spread to the public in general. I have been taught that as long as you respect the origins and ancestors of Conjure, you can practice Conjure. When talking about the practice of Conjure, the word *Conjure* will always be capitalized to make a distinction between the folk magic and the practice of conjuring spirits.

Conjure as a magical practice involves the use of the Bible. Any spell or working in this book that comes from Conjure will contain a Bible verse. In Conjure work, the Bible is viewed both as the word of God and as a magical book. Even if you do not believe in the Bible and its teachings, the Conjure spells will work for you because of the power within the Bible.

Ethical Expectations

This book contains workings from both witchcraft and Conjure practices. As the book contains both magical traditions, there will also be some baneful magic within this text. It is my belief that to understand magic the best, one needs to understand both the healing and beneficial crafts as well as the baneful crafts. By understanding baneful magic (even if we never use it), we can better protect ourselves against it and remove it when called to.

It is up to you, the reader, to decide what is and isn't ethical for you. In my practices, it is perfectly ethical to work baneful magic so long as everything else has been tried to deal with the situation. Baneful magic, while a tool and resource, is a last resort—and one that I do not take without first asking myself several questions. Asking these questions helps me to really think about the work and often helps me find other solutions to the problem.

The first question I ask myself before engaging in any sort of baneful magic is: Have I or my loved ones done anything to bring harassment, such as showing off something that triggered jealousy? If there is something that has been done, you must take ownership of said behavior. Taking ownership of behaviors prevents spells from backfiring.

The second question I ask is: Can I live with the consequences of my actions or inaction? If I can live with the action, I will do the work. If, however, I may regret acting later on, I will not cast the spell. Regretting baneful magic causes it to backfire. I once had a spell backfire on me because I started to question if it was the right thing to do. After I started to question my actions, what I wanted to happen to my target happened to me as well. This persisted until I took the time to reassess my actions and affirm I made the right choice. When it comes to baneful magic, I advise you to think hard about the actions you are about to take.

Another ethical consideration is that of controlling and dominating magic. Except for baneful magic, which is used when you are trying to stop specific behaviors, it is unethical to control the way another person thinks or acts. Using magic to have an individual think or act in a way they normally would not is disrespectful to the individual and goes against their personal will.

A Word on the Materials

The spells and workings in this text use a variety of materials. Some of the work includes the use of animal remains or leavings. Working with animal remains has been a traditional part of many magical practices. Witches and Conjure workers have always used whatever tools they have had at hand to get the work done.

The section on animal materials is included for informative purposes. Many of the animal parts mentioned can readily be found in nature. There is no reason to harm any animal for your magical practices. Only use materials that you can ethically purchase or gather from an animal that has already died. If you are uncomfortable working with animal components, you can skip that part of the work.

All the spells and formulas use dried herbal ingredients. Grinding and powdering herbal materials is easier once they have been properly dried. Some herbal materials can be found already in a ground or powdered form. Whenever possible, you should work with those forms to save yourself time, effort, and energy, which can then go elsewhere in your spellwork.

One last note: Some of the spells and formulas contain materials that could be allergens. If you or the people around you have allergies to certain materials, do not work with them. There are alternative formulas and ingredients for allergens.

It is my hope that through this book you will develop a deeper connection to the world around you. From animals to minerals and herbs, every material found within this book has its own magic to teach and offer you. Magic can be found in everything and everywhere. It can just take some time to learn how to see it and use it. Good luck and welcome to the world of magical powders.

PART I
Magical Powder Basics

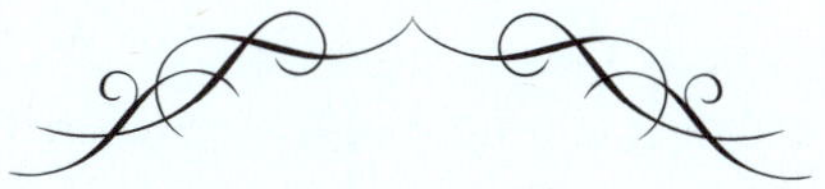

Understanding Magical Powders

Powders are not something that people often associate with witchcraft and magic. Occasionally there are references to uses of black salt for protection and that's about it, but powders are a versatile tool in magic that can be used anywhere and anytime.

One of the benefits of powders is that they can be used discreetly. For those who need to be careful about how they practice their magic and find ways to hide it, powders can be useful. Need to ward your home? Just sprinkle a protective powder of your choice around the doors and windows once a month to keep it safe.

A second benefit of working with magical powders is how they can store power. Through the creation process, these powders are infused with magical and spiritual energy. Once created, the powder will store the magic and energy within until it is needed for spellwork.

A third benefit of using magical powders is their ability to be used in multiple spells and workings. Powders can be used by themselves as a spell or included as ingredients to empower other types of spellwork. Need a filling for a sachet or spell ball? Use a magical powder. For any spell or magical working, there is a powder that can be used to add power.

Utilizing the Magic of Powders

These powders work to direct our will, desire, and intent. That's why sprinkling or applying a magical powder alone can work as a spell. The energy was gathered, charged, and stored in the powder for future use. As the powder is sprinkled, the energy and intent within it is directed and released for the spell.

Powders that are made from more than one material contain an energetic force that is a combination of all the materials used to create the powder plus mental and physical energy.

How the magic within the powder is activated will depend on the spell you are doing. For container magic, the energy is released whenever the container is worked. When used in a candle magic spell, the power is released as the candle burns. The fire from the candle heats the powder, beginning the process of releasing the stored energy.

You can even combine the use of powders and personal effects to create powerful magical works. The powder will hold the energy and essence of the spellwork while the personal effect contains the energy of that individual. Covering a personal effect or other direct representation (a photo, drawing, written name) will send that energy directly where you need it to go.

Types of Magical Powders

There are many different types of magical powders that can be utilized in your practice. Whether you are working kitchen witchery, using poppets, or performing candle magic, there is a type of magical powder that can suit your need. Each type of powder approaches the manifestation of a spell in a unique way. Different powders work best for different situations.

Witches' salt is the most well-known magical powder. As the name implies, this powder's base is salt. If there are known blocks in your path, using witches' salt is the way to go. The salt neutralizes the blocks while the other materials transform the neutralized energy into something that works for you.

Sweetening powders are another well-known type of magical powder. A sweetening powder typically uses sugar or cocoa powder as its base. The goal of a sweetening powder is to attract your goal to you quickly and to open the world to your perspective. When you need to manifest magic quickly, a sweetening powder makes the perfect addition to your spell.

Edible powders are a third type of magical powder. The thing that makes edible powders unique is that they are the only powders created exclusively from food-based materials. Edible powders are a great way to engage in kitchen magic and share your spells with those open to them.

Floor sweeps, or *dusting powders*, are a type of magical powder I learned about through my Conjure studies. This fourth type of magical powder shows the true essence of folk magic: using what's available. The use of floor sweeps is one of the ways that Conjure was able to help preserve some of the ancestral practices of enslaved people.

Two other types of magical powder are *common magical powders* and *baneful powders*. Common magical powders are magical powders that don't really fit anywhere else; they aren't a salt, a sweep, or a sweetening powder. Baneful powders are great tools to add to your magical toolbox. These powders are used strictly for baneful magic. As with all baneful magic, it is important to be careful regarding how, when, and why you use them.

There are other blends that can also work as magical powders. Herbal teas can be used the same way you would use an edible powder. Baths and washes can also be used as powders. Simply use them as is—without involving water. Powdered herbal incenses are another magical tool that can double as a powder.

Deciding What Type of Powder to Make

The following exercise can help you decide what type of magical powder you might want to make. Remember to explore and experiment. These considerations are what have worked best for me and my practice. You may find that things are different for you. At the end of the day, you should always use what works best for you and your practice.

MATERIALS

- Pen
- Paper

WORKING

1. Write down what the general intent behind the magical powder will be.
2. Ask yourself if your goal is to attract something, remove something, maintain something, or control something. Record your answer. Consider the following:
    - Attracting something lends itself to sweetening powders, common magical powders, and powdered herbal incenses. It is not uncommon

to find magnetic sand in attracting powder recipes.

- Floor sweeps work best if your goal is to remove something.
- Witches' salts, sweetening powders, and common magical powders are well suited for maintaining magical goals and use in spells that are long lasting.
- Controlling work is best done with sweetening powders or baneful powders.

3. How will the powder be used? Record your answer. Consider the following:
   - Witches' salts work best when used to charge a charm or scattered around an area to distribute the magic within it—just do not use salt-based powders in nature or you will kill any plants in the area.
   - Edible powders work best when consumed as part of the magical working.
   - Floor sweeps work best to remove and protect against energetic forces.
   - Common magical powders and baneful powders are best when they can be used as fillings for charms or part of a candle spell.
   - Sweetening powders are the most versatile of magical powders, working well by themselves, as fillings, or to charge other spells and materials.
4. What materials do you have on hand? Remember to check your spice cabinet and kitchen for spell

supplies as well as to look at what's available outside your home. Take note of the materials available and how you might use them.

5. With the answers to these questions, you can figure out what type of magical powder is best for the situation you are in.

Tools & Materials

Crafting magical powders is one of the simplest magical practices. There are very few tools required for this work. Most of the tools used can be found in your kitchen or pantry. It is this simplicity that makes the use of magical powders a practice that is available and accessible to everyone. The following is a list of tools that I use and recommend to other people.

Gloves & Masks

Some of the materials in certain magical powders should be handled with care. For safety reasons, either plastic medical gloves or gardening gloves should be utilized when dealing with those materials. You may also want to use a mask to prevent lung irritation.

Mortar & Pestle

The first tool used in crafting magical powders (aside from the curios themselves) is that of a mortar and pestle. This tool is the one that you will use to grind and pound the materials into as fine of a consistency as possible. Blenders, coffee grinders, and food processors make excellent substitutions for a mortar and pestle. If using these tools, make sure you keep your magical grinders separate from your kitchen grinders, the exception being if you are creating an edible powder.

Used Spice Jars

Old spice jars are the perfect containers to store magical powders in. Many spice jars have shaker lids. These shaker lids make it easy to apply magical powders to objects and settings. Reusing spice jars is also a great way to reduce the amount of trash that ends up in landfills, as you are providing a new use for an old container. You simply need to clean them before use. Buying new jars is also an option.

Measuring Tools

There are a variety of measuring tools that can be used when crafting magical powders. The most important and common ones would be measuring spoons and cups. These tools allow you to have precise measurements and ensure that you can replicate your formula later. To prevent cross contamination of edible versus inedible components, use a separate set of measuring tools for your magical work.

Mixing Bowl

One tool you will need is a bowl of some sort to mix your powders in. This can be anything from a plastic mixing bowl to a cauldron. I recommend against using wooden bowls, as wood is a porous material and will over time absorb the various oils. Here you will be combining both the physical materials and the energetic aspects of the powder. To prevent cross contamination, set aside a specific mixing bowl for your magical work and keep your other bowls for cooking.

Spoon or Wand

While I encourage everyone to mix some of the powder using their hands, it's not always going to be possible. Some herbs are messy, and others, such as stinging nettle and poison ivy, may cause adverse reactions. Having a spoon or wand to stir and mix the components of your powder is useful. The spoon or wand also works as a tool to help direct and focus the energetic forces as they become one united force. As with the mixing bowl and other kitchen utensils, make sure you use a different spoon for magical work than for cooking.

Food Coloring or Dye

For some magical powders, color plays a key component in the power behind the powder. Witches' salts are a great example of powders where color plays a role. When possible, the colors of your magical powders should come from the materials used, such as flowers, herbs, and crystals. In some cases, the desired colors are not easy to find in nature, so dye may be needed. There will be more information about the use of color and dye in chapter 2, "Choosing Your Materials."

Pens & Label Stickers

The last things that I include in my kit are pens and label stickers or paper and tape. I use these to label the powders I create. It is important to remember which container holds which powder. Not only can you label your powder what it is, but you can also note the date and time it was created.

Other Ingredients & Curios

When it comes to magical powders, you need to have an understanding of the materials that make them up. The ingredients in the powders determine a lot of power. This is why it is important to choose the ingredients for each powder carefully.

Herbal materials make up the bulk of the ingredients used in magical powders. Dried herbs can easily be ground into fine powders and combined with other materials. All plant matter, from flowers to roots, stems, seeds, and bark, is considered an herbal component. Note that plant thorns and bark may require the use of sandpaper to achieve a fine powder.

Animal components are some potential ingredients in magical powders. Many animals shed skin, fur, and claws. These materials can be gathered and worked with. Some animals, such as insects, can be found dead and dried. These can be ground up and used as a potent component in your magical powders.

Dirt carries power. Dirt absorbs the energy and symbolism of every action that takes place at its location. For example, bank dirt carries the energy of financial success and prosperity, while dirt from a hospital carries both healing energy and the energy of decay and death. By adding dirt to your powders, you add the power of the land to your magical works.

The final type of material that is used in crafting and creating magical powders is that of manufactured curios. These are powdered materials that do not occur in nature and are things that humans have made. Materials such as gunpowder, cornstarch, and baby powder not only add power but can make the final product easier to apply and work with.

Choosing Your Materials

The most important part of the process when creating magical powders is selecting the materials that will make up the powder. These materials will produce most of the power, and without the ingredients, there is no magical powder, just intent directed by thought and focus.

Each of your magical powders will have one base material. This is the material you will have the most of in the formula. Base materials provide the foundation the spell is built from. Along with being the foundation, your base material ties everything together.

The secondary materials and highlight materials are all chosen to support the base material. Typically, secondary materials address removing blocks, protecting your goal, and attracting your goal. Highlight or "splash flavor" materials are those such as animal remains and dirt. These have highly concentrated energy, so only a pinch or tiny portion is needed for effect.

Understanding how and why curios are used empowers you to choose the best materials for the powders you wish to make and the spell you want to perform. There are many ways to understand why curios have the correspondences that they do. The first consideration is the doctrine of signatures. After the doctrine of signatures, you have the nature of the curio, and finally, you have mythology or lore regarding the material.

Base Materials

As mentioned above, every magical powder has a base material. When crafting your powders, there is typically a three-to-one ratio of base to other materials. So, for example, if you have a total of four tablespoons of non-base materials, you will need twelve tablespoons of your base material for a total of sixteen tablespoons (or one cup) of powder.

The three-to-one ratio is a rough guide. The most important thing is that you have enough of the base that it is evenly distributed within all of the materials in your powder. Three-to-one and four-to-one ratios are common, but let your intuition and the materials you are working with guide you.

Common magical powder bases include sugar for sweetening powders and salt for witches' salts as well as sweeps. Materials such as baby powder, cat litter, and cornstarch can also be used as a base for your magical powders. A common base for cleansing and removal powder is cascarilla powder.

Cascarilla Powder

Cascarilla powder, which is made from ground chicken eggshells, is a tool from folk magic. This powder is mostly used for protection spells and cleansing work. If you add a little water to the powder, you have a chalk that can be used to trace the outline of your ritual circle.

To use the powder, you can sprinkle it along the windowsills and doorways of your home, or you can draw protective sigils on your walls using the powder as chalk. Along with cleansing, eggs can be used to remove hexes and curses, which means this powder can also be used for the same things.

You can make your own cascarilla powder by baking eggshells. This is the second easiest method of creating cascarilla powder next to working with hard-boiled eggs. All you need is parchment paper, a baking sheet or tray, your oven, and several dozen eggs, plus something to grind them with once they're dried.

Making Cascarilla Powder

This method is best for when you need a batch of cascarilla powder right away. It takes several dozen eggs to make just a small amount, so it may take a while to save the shells for what you need.

MATERIALS

- Oven
- Baking tray
- Parchment paper
- 2 to 3 dozen eggshells
- Tongs or a fork
- Oven mitt or pot holder
- Mortar and pestle or grinder of some sort
- Small container with lid
- Pen
- Sticker label

WORKING

1. Preheat the oven to 300 degrees Fahrenheit (150 degrees C).
2. Line the baking tray with the parchment paper.
3. Arrange the eggshells on the parchment paper, leaving some room between the pieces.
4. Place the baking tray in the oven for 5 minutes.
5. Using the oven mitt, take the tray out of the oven.
6. Using the tongs or fork, rotate and move the shells around so they get evenly cooked.
7. Return the tray to the oven for another 5 to 10 minutes.
8. Remove the tray from the oven and allow to cool for 30 minutes.

9. After the shells have cooled completely, carefully go through and remove any of the remaining membrane from the shells. Compost or otherwise discard this material.
10. Place the eggshells in the mortar and pestle and grind the shells until they become a fine powder.
11. Add the powder to the container for storage and label it "Cascarilla Powder." Your cascarilla powder is now ready to be used.

Correspondences & the Nature of Materials

When choosing your materials, it is important to consider the nature of the material itself. First, apply the doctrine of signatures, or the doctrine of correspondences, a belief that states that what a material looks like corresponds to what it can heal or how it can be used spiritually. This is why the herb eyebright is associated with both physical sight and spiritual or psychic sight. The flowers of the eyebright plant look like little eyes. Kudzu and ivy, as another example, gained the magical correspondence of entrapping or entangling evil due to their sprawling vines.

After you've applied the doctrine of signatures, consider other details. Scent, feel, components, natural purpose, and where the materials are found all play a role in understanding magical correspondences. Each of these factors provides insight as to how and why the materials can be used.

Once you start to look at how herbs, animals, and other materials behave and interact, you can develop a deeper connection and understanding of why they have some of the magical correspondences they do. Take roses, for example. Protection is not an obvious property of roses. They're often used to gain love, yet because of the thorns of the plant, they can be used to protect those you love and the emotion of love in general.

Applying the Doctrine of Signatures & Nature of the Material Principles

This exercise gets you to apply the doctrine of signatures to materials that you have in your home that could be used for magical work. The doctrine of signatures applies to manufactured materials as well as those materials that are found in nature.

MATERIALS

- Pen
- 2 sheets of paper
- ¼ cup (60 ml) sugar (*Saccharum officinarum*)
- ¼ cup (60 ml) vinegar
- Lists of magical correspondences (See part 3 for correspondence lists.)

WORKING

1. Write the name of this exercise at the top of all two sheets of paper.

2. Take a sheet of paper and draw a line across the center, dividing the sheet in half.
3. On the top half write "Sugar Thoughts and Observations."
4. Take the sugar in your hands. Play with the sugar. Notice how it moves. Does it flow quick or slow? Record those thoughts beneath the sugar header.
5. Taste the sugar. What does it taste like? How does it feel? Record those thoughts.
6. Write down any other thoughts you have regarding the sugar, such as how it's used and why you use it.
7. On the bottom half of the same sheet of paper, write "Vinegar Thoughts and Observations."
8. Repeat steps 4 through 6 with the vinegar.
9. Using your correspondence table references, look at the magical correspondences associated with sugar.
10. Look back at your observations of sugar. On the sheet of paper, circle the observations or correspondences that are the same on your list and this book's. Underline the observations or correspondences that are different.
11. Repeat steps 9 and 10 with the vinegar.
12. On the top half of the second sheet of paper, write out the underlined correspondences for sugar. Under each of the underlined words or

phrases, which came from only your observations, write where that association comes from and why you have that. Reflect.

13. On the bottom half of the second sheet of paper, repeat step 12 for vinegar.
14. Now that you have tried this with two very different magical materials that I selected for you, go ahead and try this exercise with other materials you work with. This will help you see how many of your correspondences align with traditional uses and which ones come solely from your personal experiences.

The Importance of Lore

Another factor that comes into play when establishing traditional and modern magical correspondences is the lore associated with materials. When it comes to magical work, lore includes folk remedies, ritual uses, application in myths, and use in legends. Every culture has its own rituals, legends, and myths, which is one of the reasons why there are so many different magical correspondences across the world. By looking at lore, you can see how different people and cultures may have worked with various materials, which provides the how and why for materials' many uses.

The Bible

Throughout the Bible are multiple examples of herbs and animal curios being used for ritual or magical work. This is one of the reasons why I consider the Bible a magical text as much as a mythological text. Lore about the cleansing and protection power of the herb hyssop (*Hyssopus officinalis*) comes from the Bible. The story states:

> *Take a bunch of hyssop, dip it into the blood in the basin and put some of the blood on the top and on both sides of the doorframe. None of you shall go out of the door of your house until morning. When the Lord goes through the land to strike down the Egyptians, he will see the blood on the top and sides of the doorframe and will pass over that doorway, and he will not permit the destroyer to enter your houses and strike you down.*[1]

The Old Testament is not the only place where herbal correspondence can be found. One of my favorite bits of herbal lore comes from the Gospel of Matthew, where there's a discussion about the importance of letting faith live and grow naturally. The Mark 13:31–32 states:

> *He told them another parable: "The kingdom of heaven is like a mustard seed, which a man took and planted in his field. Though it is the smallest of all seeds, yet when it grows, it is the largest of garden*

1. Exodus 12:22–23.

plants and becomes a tree, so that the birds come and perch in its branches."[2]

Greek Mythology

Greek mythology is full of herbal lore. One example that is often forgotten is how the herbs within the mint family have an association with the underworld. This connection stems from the myth where Persephone transforms the nymph Minthe into a plant as punishment for seducing Hades.

Another association from Greek mythology is that of the herb marjoram with joy, lust, and desire. In ancient Greece and Rome, newly married couples would wear a wreath of marjoram to bring them joy, happiness, and love.

Finding Lore

This exercise gives you practice in reading materials and finding the magical lore associated with curios. If there is no physical Bible to be found in your home, I highly recommend using the website BibleGateway. It has multiple translations available to read and explore. Please note that the list of Bible verses found within this exercise is not exhaustive; there are numerous herbs and correspondences that can be found in the Bible.

2. Matthew 13:31–32.

MATERIALS

- Bible (any translation)
- Pen
- 1 to 3 sheets of paper
- A magical herbal reference guide (I recommend *Cunningham's Encyclopedia of Magical Herbs*.)

WORKING

1. On one sheet of paper, make a list of the following Bible verses. Each one mentions at least one herb. The verses are listed in their biblical book order.
    - Genesis 30:14–16
    - Numbers 11:4–9
    - Psalm 51:7
    - Isaiah 28:23–28
    - Matthew 23:23–24
    - Luke 11:42
2. Once you've written down each verse, read through them and list the herbs mentioned. Leave space under each of the verses and herbs; you will need room to write down correspondences.
3. Next to each herb, write down what correspondences you believe can be inferred from the Bible verse.
4. Use the magical herbal reference guide to look up the herbs listed and see if the magical correspondences you came up with are listed or not. Circle the correspondences on your list that are

similar, related, or connected. Underline the correspondences that are different.

5. Under each of the underlined words, which came from your observations reading the Bible, expand on where that association came from and why you have that. Know that neither list is right nor wrong.

Color & Dye

The last element to consider when choosing materials for your magical powders is that of color. By using colors with energies that correspond to the work at hand, you are adding the power of that light energy to your magic.

This is where food coloring is often applied in the creation of magical powders. I personally have only used food coloring for my blue and purple witches' salts. If you know how to make dyes using natural materials and wish to keep your products all natural, use those methods instead. In my own experience, I have not had any issues with dyed materials. I have simply found that dyed materials have more power due to the light energy.

The following is a list of my color correspondences. I use these correspondences in basically all the magical work that I do, including my healing work. Color helps me focus on my intent manifesting. Experiment with these correspondences and see what works for you.

Red: Desire, fire, love, passion, protection, renewal, sex

Red-Orange: Desire, life, lust, rebirth through destruction, sexuality

Orange: Desire, drive, energy, fire, passion

Gold: Divinity, fertility, the goddess Sif, the Horned God of Wicca, money, success, wheat

Yellow: Alarms/warning, life, money, success, summer, sun

Lime Green: Cleansing, good luck, refreshing

Green: Healing, life, money, prosperity, success

Turquoise: Healing, peace, relaxation, success, water

Blue: Cleansing, healing, health, water, wellness

Violet: Meditation, psychic development, spirit sight

Indigo: Astral travel, psychic development, spirituality

Black: Banishment, death, protection, removal, underworld

Brown: Animals, earth, fertility, protection, strength, trees

Rust: Age, decay, removal

Pink: Friendship, innocence, peace, self-love

Silver: Beauty, feminine divinity, luck, the moon goddess of Wicca, money, prosperity

White/Clear: Innocence, potential for everything, purity

Color Association

The following exercise provides a way for you to develop your own relationship with the energy and power of color. As with herbs and curios, it is important to create your own associations with colors. You will have more power and confidence in your work using your own associations over the standard ones. For best results, you may want to record yourself reading this exercise's meditation to play back later, or you may want to have someone read the meditation for you.

MATERIALS

- Pen
- 3 pieces of paper
- Recording device, optional

WORKING

1. On the first sheet of paper, write a list of colors, leaving space between each color for additional writing.
2. Go back over the list and in the space under each color, write down what you think of and associate with that color. Include emotions, locations, ideas, and images.
3. Set the list aside, then sit down and get comfortable. When you are ready, listen to the following meditation:

   Close your eyes and relax. Inhale slowly through the count of four. Hold your breath for the count of four and then exhale for four counts. Repeat three times. Take a deep breath and slowly exhale. As you exhale, release all the tension in your

body. Feel the tension release from your neck, shoulders, and arms, through your core, and finally down your legs and feet. Slowly begin to count back from thirteen to one, visualizing the numbers as you count down. When you reach one, you have reached a gentle and light meditative state.

Begin to count back from twelve to one, this time without seeing the numbers. Relax and feel yourself enter a deeper meditative state. When you reach one, a large screen appears before you. This is the screen of your mind. A brilliant white light streams from the screen and surrounds you.

You find that you have been transported to a fountain of rainbow energy. As you look at the fountain, you can see that each color is its own stream of liquid light. They are all simply flowing together to create the rainbow illusion.

As you walk through the lights, you can feel the unique vibrations of each color. You start with red and walk through the stream of light, letting the light surround you and fill you. As the light envelops you, take notice of all images, sensations, and feelings you experience. Hold on to those experiences.

Now you walk to the next stream. This stream of light is red-orange. You walk through the stream of red-orange light.

Let the light surround you and fill you. As the light surrounds you take notice of all images, sensations, and feelings you experience. Hold on to those experiences.

Now you walk to the next stream. The next stream of light is orange. You walk through the stream of orange light, letting the light surround you and fill you. As the light envelops you, take notice of all images, sensations, and feelings you experience. Hold on to those experiences.

The next stream of light is yellow. You walk through the stream of yellow light, letting the light surround you and fill you. As the light envelops you, take notice of all images, sensations, and feelings you experience. Hold on to those experiences.

The next stream of light is green. You walk through the stream of green light, letting the light surround you and fill you. As the light envelops you, take notice of all images, sensations, and feelings you experience. Hold on to those experiences.

The next stream of light is blue. You walk through the stream of blue light, letting the light surround you and fill you. As the light envelops you, take notice of all images, sensations, and feelings you experience. Hold on to those experiences.

The next stream of light is purple. You walk through the stream of purple light, letting the light surround you and fill you. As the light envelops you, take notice of all images, sensations, and feelings you experience. Hold on to those experiences.

Now you walk to the next stream. The next stream of light is silver. You walk through the stream of silver light, letting the light surround you and fill you. As the light envelops you, take notice of all images, sensations, and feelings you experience. Hold on to those experiences.

The next stream of light is gold. You walk through the stream of gold light, letting the light surround you and fill you. As the light envelops you, take notice of all images, sensations, and feelings you experience. Hold on to those experiences.

The next stream of light is brown. You walk through the stream of brown light, letting the light surround you and fill you. As the light envelops you, take notice of all images, sensations, and feelings you experience. Hold on to those experiences.

You come to the last two streams of light. The first stream is black light. You walk through the stream of black light, letting the light surround you and fill you. As the light envelops you, take notice of all images, sensations, and feelings you experience. Hold on to those experiences.

> *The last stream is pure white light. You walk through the stream of white light, letting the light surround you and fill you. As the light envelops you, take notice of all images, sensations, and feelings you experience. Hold on to those experiences.*
>
> *When you reach the edge of the river of light, you see the same bright light as before. It sends you back to the screen of your mind. Walk back through the screen and begin to count up from one to twelve. When you reach twelve, begin to wiggle your toes and fingers. Now count up from one to thirteen. When you reach thirteen, open your eyes. Stretch your body. You have returned to normal waking consciousness.*

4. Place your hands on the floor. Direct any excess energy you have from the meditation into the earth.
5. Record your experiences for each color on the second piece of paper. Use these experiences and associations to build and develop your personal color correspondence chart on the final sheet of paper. Be sure to take notice of where your preconceptions and experiences come from and how your list differs from the list I gave you.

Building Personal Relationships

As I noted at the beginning of the last exercise, your personal relationship with a material is just as important as the traditional lore and correspondence—if not more. The more you work with a material, the stronger your relationship with that material will become.

One of the best ways to establish a relationship with a material is to align your spiritual vibrations with that of the material. When we align our energetic vibrations with the vibrations of a curio, the energy within the curio responds and will start to resonate. As your energy and the energy of the curio align, you can claim the power of the curio as your own.

Vibration Alignment

In this exercise you will align your energy with the energy of a curio you hold in your hands, allowing you to create a deeper relationship and understanding of that material. For best results, repeat this exercise multiple times with the same curio before trying another material. When it comes to selecting your curio, I recommend using a crystal such as jasper or an herb such as lavender (*Lavandula officinale*).

Materials

- Curio
- Pen
- Paper

WORKING

1. Get into a comfortable seated position. Take several breaths to relax and center yourself. When you are calm and centered, you can begin.
2. Hold the curio in your dominant hand.
3. Close your eyes and begin to chant the following:

   I vibrate in harmony with (insert curio here).

4. Continue to chant while holding the curio. After a little while, you will begin to feel your body vibrating at a different energetic level than it was before. Keep the chant going until you can no longer feel a difference between your vibrations and the vibrations of the material being held. When this happens, it means the vibrations from your mind and body have aligned and are at the same frequency as the curio. Take note of any sensations you have. Remember any images that you get while holding this vibration alignment. Remember the sensation.
5. Place the curio down and thank it. Release the vibrations in your body by directing them down your legs into the earth.
6. Record your experiences.
7. Next time you are going to use that curio in a spell or magical working, recall the vibrations you felt during this exercise and bring them forward. You can now direct that energy into whatever magical work you have planned.

Final Considerations

Aside from choosing materials corresponding to your primary intent, there are a few things to consider when building your formula. Do you need protection? If so, you may want to include a material that relates to protecting your goal.

Are there blocks in your way? If so, you may want to include materials that are good at opening doors and breaking down blocks. This is where cleansing and removal materials might be used.

Are you trying to attract or remove something from your life? Deciding if you are going to attract or remove something will also help further determine the materials you select.

Choosing Your Materials

The following exercise gives you practice in selecting materials for your magical works. When performing this exercise, it may be handy to have an encyclopedia of magical correspondences or similar resource on hand. For the sake of this exercise, we will work with protection curios.

MATERIALS

- Materials that correspond to the work at hand (i.e., protection)
- Pendulum or other form of yes/no divination

WORKING

1. Place the potential powder materials in a row.
2. Using your divination tool, ask if that material is right for the magic at hand. If the answer is yes, put the material aside and move on to the next one. When the answer is no, set that item aside in a second pile. If you get maybe as an answer, create a pile of maybes.
3. Repeat step 2 with any maybe materials until you have a clear set of yes and no curios.
4. Take the selection of yes materials. Hold the your divination tool over each one and ask if that material is to be used in your formula. Continue the process until you have three to five ingredients for your magical powder.

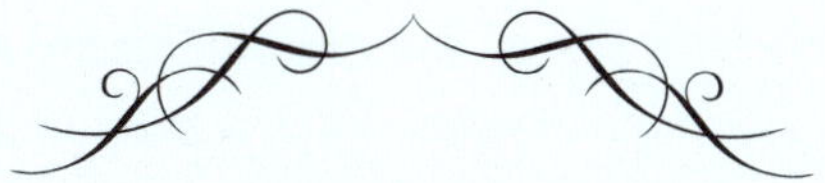

Creating the Powder & Casting the Spell

Magical powders are such an effective tool because this new energetic form has been created for one job: manifesting your intent. Every step in the process of creating a magical powder is essential, as they all play into creating the final energetic and spiritual shape of the powder. Every step adds a different energetic component.

Components of Magical Powders

There are four different types of energy that combine to create the essence and power behind a magical powder. Most of the power in a magical powder comes from the spiritual essence of the curios chosen, as I have already discussed. Mental, emotional, and physical energy are the three other types of energy.

Spiritual Energy

Everything contains energy and spirit. When we work magic, we simply learn to tap into the hidden energy of the world. That spiritual energy is then manipulated and shaped into a form suitable for the job at hand. Most of the energy for the magical powder will come from the spiritual essence found within the individual ingredients that make up the powder.

Mental Energy

Mental energy comes from focusing and concentrating on your intent. This includes any visualizations you have; it all adds your mental energy to the spell. Intent is the base of your magic. Your intent is simply your goal or what you want to achieve from your spell. What change are you trying to bring about in your life? The more power behind your intent, the more powerful your spell becomes.

Will-Working Mental Projection

This exercise illustrates just how much energy is used when concentrating and focusing on a specific goal or intent. For best results, start with something simple, such as finding the best parking space or not having any traffic when running late.

MATERIALS

- Pen
- Paper

EXERCISE

1. Sit in a comfortable position. Take a deep breath and relax. Inhale deeply and hold for four counts. Exhale for four counts. Inhale four counts and hold for four counts. Exhale four counts. Inhale four counts. Hold for four counts and exhale for four counts.

2. Take a breath and truly relax your body. Begin by relaxing your muscles, starting at your head and neck and moving down through your shoulders and into your arms. From your arms, relax your chest and core, moving down to your thighs and calves and into your feet. Tighten and release your toes and ankles. Feel your body become light and calm.

3. Focus and concentrate on a specific goal or desire you have. As you focus on that goal, think about how you will feel when that goal has manifested. See and feel as if that goal has already manifested in your life. Know that your intent, goal, or desire will manifest. Hold on to these images and feelings as long as possible. Take note of how your body feels while focusing and concentrating.

4. When you can no longer hold on to the images, feelings, and sensations, raise your dominant hand and extend two fingers out to the world.

5. Release the images and energy from your mind, and direct the energy through your arm and out those fingers into the universe. Know that this

energy is being sent out to manifest your goal and desire.

6. Write about your experience. Include if you lost focus at any time and how you felt before, during, and after the experience.

Emotional Energy

Your emotions can be tapped into while crafting magical powders to empower your intent. The more emotional the desire behind your intent, the more intense your intent is likely to be. Directing the intense power of your emotions into your spellwork is a safe way to release and express those emotions.

Physical Energy

Physical energy refers to the power of the physical actions involved in the creation of your magical powder. These add your energy into your work. Be mindful of just how much physical energy you use in your spellwork. If you use too much energy, you will drain yourself physically and may be unable to do other tasks.

When you use some of your physical energy in this way, it is important to recover and replace it. The key is to eat something that can be digested quickly that contains sugar, protein, and salt. I often eat chocolate, peanut butter, or nuts to help me ground and recover the energy expended.

Making the Powders

Crafting magical powders is a fairly simple process. As with all magical work, the first step is always knowing what your intent is—what you are trying to achieve using this magic. Once you know what your goal or intent is, it drives the selection of the curios and other materials for your powder. With the curios selected, it is time to activate them.

After the spirits are woken up, you can begin to play with energy. This is where you tap into or access the energy stored within the materials.

After awakening the curios and playing with the energy, you have the physical process of grinding the curios into a powdered form. This is where your physical energy gets combined with spiritual energy from the curio. While grinding, focus on your intent and direct that energy down into the material, programming or charging the material with its purpose in the powder.

Mixing, shaking, and stirring all the materials is the last part of the process. This is where the individual materials and energetic forces become blended into one new energetic force, creating a new spirit. That spirit is the spirit of the powder.

Awakening & Activating the Curios

Before your ingredients can do any work for you, they need to wake up. Until the forces within the materials are woken up and activated, no energy will flow from the curios. The energy is simply there and exists. When we wake up the spirits within, we can tap into their power and create magic.

There are many ways you can activate and wake a spirit. Some people use their breath to wake spirits, and others use offerings of water or alcohol. In my personal practice, I use my breath and a meditative technique to align with the energy. Once I feel that the energy is flowing and activated, I can begin to channel the energy toward the work at hand.

Formal rituals are an excellent way to call on the power of spirits. One of the reasons it works so well is that you are in a sacred space, which means you are protected by the gods and spirits within the space. Using a sacred place brings you closer to the spiritual realm, making it easier to communicate with the spirits.

Activation of Energy

In this exercise, you will learn to sense the energy of a material and how to activate it for your magical work. This exercise can be applied to any material that you work with in your spellcraft. For best results, perform the exercise multiple times with a single material—before trying the next material. I recommend trying the exercise with an herb such as lavender (*Lavandula officinalis*) or catnip (*Nepeta cataria*) or a stone such as onyx or obsidian. If alcohol is unavailable, use clean, fresh water in its place.

MATERIALS

- Herb, crystal, or other curio you want to activate
- Shot of rum or other alcohol
- Pen
- Paper

WORKING

1. Begin by getting yourself into a light meditative state using your preferred method. Light any incense and play any soft music that you use when you do meditation work.
2. Take your chosen material and hold it in your hand. Take a deep breath and exhale over the material. As you exhale, state:

   I awaken you, spirit of (insert curio here).

3. Tap the curio three times. Then take another deep breath, exhaling over the curio.
4. Take your finger and dip it into the alcohol. Rub the alcohol on the curio. As you rub the alcohol on the curio, state:

   I feed you today, for the magic you send my way.

5. You should start to feel a pulse of energy from the curio as the spirit wakes up and gets ready to do work. As the force within the curio begins to wake up, take note of any sensations you receive. Notice any emotions, images, and feelings

coming from the curio. Write down these experiences. Those images and feelings could lead to deepening your understanding of the material.

Awakening Spirits Ceremony

This simple ritual can be used to wake up the spirits of any curio that you work with. For best results, perform this ritual working with one curio at a time. This allows your bond with the curio to strengthen. The stronger your relationship with a curio, the more power it will give you. If alcohol is unavailable, use clean, fresh water in its place.

MATERIALS

- Altar table
- Altar cloth
- Bowl holding the herb, crystal, or other curio you want to activate
- Taper candleholder
- White taper candle
- Bowl of water
- Shot glass
- Rum or other alcohol
- Broom
- Lighter or matches
- 1 tablespoon (15 ml) salt
- Wand or spoon
- Notebook
- Pen

WORKING

1. Prepare the altar with the bowl with the curio in the center. Place the candleholder in front of and to the right of the bowl. Secure the candle in it. Place the bowl of water directly across from the candleholder. Set the shot glass behind the bowl and place the alcohol under or beside the altar.
2. Using the broom, sweep the perimeter of the ritual area, moving in a clockwise manner. As you walk and sweep, know that all unwanted energy is being moved away. Only that which you need remains.
3. When you have walked the perimeter at least twice and feel that it has been cleansed, set the broom down.
4. Light the candle. As you light the candle, state:

   Candle burning bright, illuminate this rite.

5. Pick up the candleholder and carefully hold it as you walk the perimeter of the circle. While walking the circle with the candle, state:

   By the sacred power of fire, this space is cleansed by my desire.

6. Place the candleholder and candle back on the altar.
7. Sprinkle the salt into the water. Use the wand or spoon to stir the salt into the water until it's dissolved. While stirring the salt, state:

> ***Creature of salt, neutralize all that which should not be here. Cleanse this space that sacred spiritual communication may take place here.***

8. Pick up the bowl of water and walk the perimeter of your ritual area. Sprinkle the water as you walk, stating:

   By this blessed water, this space is cleansed and protected.

9. Set the bowl of water back down on the altar.
10. Pick up the bowl containing the material you are trying to wake up, and pass the bowl safely over the candle flame. As you do so, state:

    Spirit of (material in the bowl), I bring you fire, warmth, and life.

11. Now hold the bowl containing the material over the water. State:

    Spirit of (material in the bowl), I present you with water, that you may be nourished.

12. Sit down facing the altar. Place the bowl in your lap. Hold your hands over the bowl. State:

    Spirit of (material in the bowl), I welcome you today. I invite you to join me in my magical work on this day.

13. When you feel the material's energy buzzing and activated, set the bowl back down on the altar.
14. Fill the shot glass with alcohol. State:

Spirit, I offer you this drink today. May we work together to create powerful magic.

15. Sit and communicate with the spirit of the curio. Take note of any thoughts, feelings, and images you receive while focusing on the curio.
16. When you can no longer sense the spirit of the curio, thank the spirit for its time and extinguish the candle.
17. Record any messages and experiences you had while communicating with the curio.

Charging the Material

With the spirit awake and activated, it is now time to charge the material and give it work to do. All the actions that you have taken to this point have helped you feel and sense the energy of each material as it exists. Now it is time to shape the energy and give it a job. This process is called charging or programing.

Using Your Voice

Words have power. Saying chants, reciting prayers, and speaking affirmations are all ways that the power of words can be used to direct your energy—mental, emotional, and physical—and charge your magical work. As the words are repeated, energy is raised. This is also how reciting Bible passages or prayers to specific saints and spirits can be useful in your magical work.

The following exercise is used to illustrate how using words impacts the energetic feel of the curios you work with.

Charging by Voice

For this exercise we are looking at bringing strength and protection into our lives by charging a stone. The chant we will use to charge this stone is the Prayer to Saint Michael. The Prayer to Saint Michael is one of my favorite protection prayers to work with.

MATERIALS

- Small palm stone or tumble (labradorite, obsidian, jasper, or onyx is recommended) (for protection)
- Pen
- Paper

WORKING

1. Hold the stone in your receptive hand.
2. On the paper, make a note of what the stone feels like before you charge it. Include emotions, images, sensations, and anything else that comes to your mind as you focus on the stone in its natural state.
3. Close your eyes and take a breath. Focus on turning this stone into a protective charm.
4. Once you are centered, open your eyes and begin to recite the Prayer to Saint Michael:

> ***Saint Michael the Archangel, defend us in battle, be our protection against the wickedness and snares of the devil. May God rebuke him we humbly pray; and do thou, O Prince of the Heavenly host, by the power of God, cast into hell Satan and all the evil spirits who prowl about the world seeking the ruin of souls. Amen.***[3]

5. Repeat the prayer five to seven times, directing all of the energy into the stone.
6. Now make notes about how the stone feels after being charged by the prayer. Be sure to observe the differences in energetic sensations before and after charging the crystal.

Charging Powders & Shaping the Energy

Charging magical powders is the most crucial step when crafting and working with them. When you charge and focus on the energy of curios, you program them with what it is you want them to do. By telling the spirits what you want from them, they can provide you with energy that aligns with your goal.

When you charge the materials, you can take the different raw energetic frequencies and transform them into a single cohesive energy. There are many ways to charge and draw out the specific energy needed. Focusing on your

3. Prayer to St. Michael the Archangel.

intent is the primary way materials are charged. As we discussed earlier, this can be done chanting words and phrases.

Once the materials have their individual charge, it is time to blend everything together. This is where you will not only combine the physical components but the energetic components as well.

Importance of Charging Each Material Individually

When it comes to charging the materials, it is essential that each curio be charged individually. Charging each of the materials individually allows you to gradually build the form and shape of the final spirit. You are better able to blend the different energetic forces together by adding them one at a time rather than trying to mix them all at once.

Charging the items one at a time and slowly mixing them also layers the energy in the magic much more effectively. When all the materials are distributed evenly in the powder, the energetic forces are also distributed evenly. I have found that adding all the materials at once leaves the powder with an uneven distribution of materials and energy.

Now all of the energy and spiritual forces have become something new. This new spirit now exists in the powder to do whatever work it is you gave it

Crafting Powders

When you look at the individual components, it seems that crafting and creating magical powders is a lot of work. The truth is that it *is* work. All spells take work and effort. The process may seem intimidating, but it's not that bad. Taking your time at first gives you practice in sensing and feeling the differences in energy. As you make more powders and perform more spells, you will be able to find techniques and tricks that work best for you. For now, simply follow the process as best you can—more effort, more power.

The following ritual shows how all the exercises come together in the formal process to create a magical powder.

The Creation of a Magical Powder

In this example ritual, we will create a sweeten luck powder.

MATERIALS

- Worktable
- Tablecloth
- Mixing bowl
- Mortar and pestle
- Spoon or wand
- Materials for Sweeten Luck Powder (See chapter 7, "Sweetening Magical Powders," for the formula.)
- Small container with lid
- Pen
- Sticker label

WORKING

1. Set the tablecloth on top of your workspace. In the center, place the mixing bowl. Put the mortar and pestle to the right of your mixing bowl. Place the materials for the powder around the bowl.
2. Pick up your base material and activate the spirit.
3. If the curio needs to be ground or powdered, set the curio in the mortar and pestle. If the curio is already in a ground or powdered form, place it in the mixing bowl and skip to step 6. Once you've added all the curios, proceed to step 9.
4. Use the mortar and pestle to grind the material into as fine a powder as you can. While you are grinding the curio, focus on the intent behind the powder. Hold on to the thoughts, images, emotions, and physical sensations you have regarding your intent for as long as you possibly can.
5. When you can no longer hold on to that intent and the curio has been ground as finely as possible, release that energy from your mind and body into the powder. Use the spoon or wand to move the materials from the mortar and pestle into the mixing bowl.
6. Use the spoon to stir the materials together. This starts building and creating the new spirit of the powder.
7. Once they are thoroughly combined, repeat steps 3 through 6 for each remaining material. As each

material is added, the energy from that item is mixed in with the materials before it.

8. Once all the materials have been mixed and the energy has been blended as evenly as possible, use the spoon to fill the storage container with the powder.
9. Label the powder and place it in storage. Any excess powder that does not fit in your container can be used immediately.

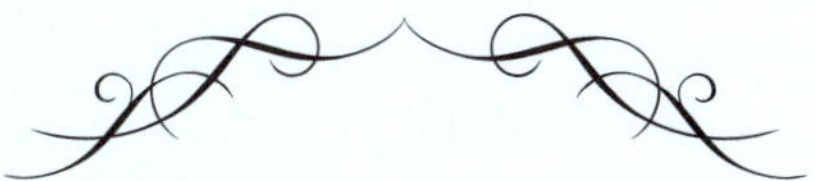

Storing, Feeding & Recharging Your Powder

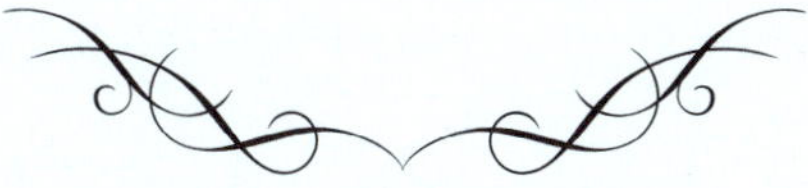

One of the best things about working with magical powders is that a powder stores its magical energy until it is called upon and used. Once a powder has been made, its charge remains effective for many months. I have even found the energy and power within my powders still potent three or more years later. The best way to ensure that your powder retains its energy is to make sure you engage in proper storage.

When you seal the storage container, you lock in the spirit and magical power. Until the powder is used in a working, the spirit within the powder remains dormant and asleep. These spirits can remain dormant and effective as long as they are kept away from heat, light, and moisture.

A Warning About Improper Storage

Your powders' storage location should be dry because moisture causes physical damage to powders. Mold is a product of exposure to water or moisture. When food becomes moldy, it has begun to decay. Finding mold in your magical powders is no different than finding mold anywhere else. It needs to be thrown out. Any magical or spiritual charges and forces that were in your powder have since died. Only decay remains.

When magical powders are exposed to heat or sunlight, the energy stored within diminishes. Sunlight absorbs energy. By keeping your powders in a place where sunlight can reach them, you are inviting the sunlight to absorb the energy within the powder, returning that energy to the universe.

Preventing damage to your powders from light, heat, or moisture is easy enough: You simply need to store your powders in a place that is dark, dry, and cool. I store my powders in a plastic bin that is covered with a blanket or piece fabric to keep the sunlight out.

Proper Storage

Proper storage begins with your choice of storage container. The type of container you use is going to be based on physical storage space, availability of materials, cost of materials, and volume of powders created and produced.

Baggies

When storage space is a concern, plastic sandwich baggies (the kind that seal closed) can be used to store your powders. Plastic baggies are inexpensive, easy to obtain, and take up little room. Baggies are also easy to transport.

One downside is that the baggies can tear easily. It's a good idea to make sure that wherever you store your magical powders, there are no sharp objects or other items that could poke holes in a bag. Tearing easily also makes it difficult to change labels or fix labeling mistakes.

Plastic baggies are not environmentally friendly. When using plastic baggies to store your powders, try to reuse the baggies for as long as possible. By reusing plastic baggies, you can reduce the amount of trash you create.

Glass & Plastic Jars

Small glass and plastic jars, including old spice containers, work great for storing magical powders. For one thing, these jars are often clear, allowing you to see what powder is in the container. Many spice jars come with shaker lids. These lids make it easy to dispense the magical powders.

Prepping & Reusing Containers

Any container that is fresh (i.e., being used for the first time) does not require any prep. These containers can simply be picked up, opened, and used. No washing or cleansing is necessary. Containers that are being reused, however, do require a little prep.

Prepping a container for your magical powder is a simple process. The container just needs to be washed and cleansed. Washing the container ensures that whatever was in the container previously is completely removed. This means there will be no contamination with other materials or forces.

While you clean the container, focus on the container being cleansed and the last use being removed. Just wash with hot, soapy water and rinse and dry thoroughly. It is essential for the container to be completely dry before use. If the container is not completely dry, you risk mold developing.

At some point, you will eventually run out of your magical powder and need to create a fresh batch. The best way to ensure that your powders maintain a consistent quality is to use the same containers for the same powders. By using the same container repeatedly, the container will eventually maintain a residual magical charge. The residual energy will help keep your magical powder charged while in storage.

If a container needs to be used for a new type of magical powder (e.g., going from a money powder to a healing powder), the container must first be washed and cleansed. Cleansing the containers between magical powders prevents energetic contamination. Energetic contamination makes magical powders less effective.

Powder Container Prep

Use this simple and effective ritual to wash and cleanse containers between magical uses.

MATERIALS

- Wash basin
- Hot water
- Liquid dish soap
- Small bowl
- Tea ball, cheesecloth, or muslin drawstring bag
- ½ tablespoon (7 ml) hyssop (*Hyssopus officinalis*) (for cleansing, removal)
- ½ tablespoon (7 ml) lemongrass (*Cymbopogon citratus*) (for cleansing, removal)
- ½ tablespoon (7 ml) salt (for cleansing, neutralization)
- Dish sponge
- Container to be washed
- Towel or cloth

WORKING

1. Fill the wash basin with hot water.
2. Add three drops of liquid dish soap.
3. In the small bowl combine the hyssop, lemongrass, and salt.

4. Fill the tea ball, cheesecloth, or muslin bag with the hyssop, lemongrass, and salt. Place the bag in the wash basin.
5. Use the sponge to wash the container and remove all previous contents. As you wash the container, repeat the following chant three to five times:

   Wash away, cleanse today. That which was here before must now go away.

6. Rinse the container under clean, fresh water.
7. Use the towel or cloth to dry the container thoroughly, removing all the moisture. The clean and dry container is now ready to be used.

Feeding the Spirit of Your Powder

Even when the forces within a powder are sealed in a container, as time passes, some energy escapes and returns to the universe. To keep your magical powder going, you must feed it new energy. This energy needs to come from both physical and mental sources in order to keep the powder charged.

To feed your powder, play with it by running your fingers through the mixture, feeling its energy. While doing so, think about why you created this powder. As you reflect on that base charge and intent, focus and direct that mental energy through your fingers into the powder. The physical action and mental focus will feed the spirit fresh energy, keeping the spirit alive.

In addition to playing with your magical powder, there are other ways that you can feed it. Physically shaking the container that your powder is in is an excellent way to recharge it. When I shake my powders, I also recite a chant or mantra related to the original base charge.

Anointing the lid of the container with an oil charged with the same or a similar intent will also feed the spirit. As the lid gets anointed, the energy from the oil travels into the contents of the container, feeding the forces within. Passing the container through incense smoke works the same way; the powder is just being fed with air and smoke instead of a liquid.

Magical powders should be fed at least once a week. The more you play with and work the container holding the powder, the more powerful and effective the magic will be. In addition to feeding the powder, simply using the powder helps keep the spirit alive and active.

Feeding Your Magical Powder

This exercise is here to help you find the best way to feed your magical powders. Magic is unique to each of us; knowing what actions work best for you will help you achieve the best results. You will not be able to perform this exercise until you have made three different magical powders. You can find recipes in part 2. Incense formulas can be found in part 3.

MATERIALS

- 3 different magical powders
- Bowl
- Paper
- Pen
- Spoon or wand
- Charcoal disc
- Long-stemmed lighter
- Tongs
- Censer (with salt or sand in the base to protect against heat damage)
- Incense
- Anointing oil that matches the intent of one magical powder

EXERCISE

1. Dump the first magical powder into the bowl.
2. Take this magical powder in your hand and make a note of how it feels energetically. Write down what you experience and feel.
3. Run your fingers through the magical powder. As you run your fingers through it, think about the goal behind the powder and imagine that goal manifesting in your life. Direct the energy from any images, emotions, sensations, or feelings you receive through your hands into the magical powder.

4. Make a note of how the powder feels energetically.
5. Use the spoon or wand to return the powder to its container.
6. Pick up the second magical powder. Make a note of how it feels energetically. Write down what you experience.
7. Use the tongs to hold the charcoal in one hand. With the other hand, use the long-stemmed lighter to light the charcoal. When the edges of the charcoal are glowing, carefully place the charcoal in the censer.
8. Sprinkle enough of the incense over the piece of charcoal so there is smoke.
9. Pass the container of the second powder through the incense smoke five times, reciting a mantra or chant related to your original intent.
10. Take note of how the energy of the magical powder feels compared to when you first picked it up in step 6. Record the experiences.
11. Pick up the third magical powder. Make a note of how it feels energetically. Write down what you experience.
12. Take the anointing oil and anoint the container of the third magical powder. While you anoint the container, make a statement of intent based on the type of powder (healing, money, luck, etc.) you are recharging.

13. Take note of how the energy of the magical powder feels compared to when you first picked it up in step 11. Record the experiences.
14. Extinguish the incense and let it cool. While the censer and charcoal cool, look over the results of steps 4, 10, and 13. The method that had the most intense result in being fed is the method you should use going forward to feed your magical powders.
15. Once the charcoal disc and censer have cooled, dispose of the charcoal and incense. Return everything else to its original storage place.

Honoring the Spirit of Your Magical Powder

When you craft magical powders, you create a new spirit. This spirit exists and lives within the powder you made. Just as the energy of the powder needs to be fed and recharged, the spirit within the powder needs to be honored and respected.

Honoring the spirit of your magical powder is no different than honoring any other spirit you work with. Giving the spirit gifts of energy through burning incense and saying prayers is the primary and most effective way I know to honor any spirit. Honoring the spirit of your magical powder should always be done, even when you are not actively using the powder.

By honoring the spirit of the powder outside of working with the powder, you show the spirit that you respect it as a spiritual life form. Showing that respect increases the amount of power the spirit will be willing to give to you when you do use the powder.

Simple Spirit Veneration Ritual

This is a simple ritual that can be altered to suit specific spirits. Simply change the incense or add an appropriate secondary incense to match the chosen spirit. This working is inspired by Wicca-style rituals, but it can be altered to work with other traditions and practices.

In this sample ritual, we will venerate the spirit of a black salt powder. The formulas for black salts can be found in the chapter "Witches' Salts."

Materials

- Small table
- Altar cloth
- Plate
- The magical powder being honored
- White pillar candle
- Bowl of salt
- Tea light candleholder
- White tea light candle
- Heat-resistant pad
- Censer (with salt or sand in the base to protect against heat damage)
- Bowl of water

- Tongs
- Charcoal disc
- Long-stemmed lighter
- Generic Ritual Blessings Incense (Recipe can be found in part 3.)

WORKING

1. Cover the table with the cloth to protect your workspace.
2. In the center of the table, place the plate. Set the white pillar candle on the plate. Behind the plate, place the bowl of salt. Directly behind the bowl of salt, place the container of the magical powder being honored. To the right of the plate, place the tea light candleholder and the tea light candle. In front of the plate, place the heat-resistant pad and censer. Finally, place the bowl of water to the left of the plate.
3. Use the tongs to hold the piece of charcoal and light it with the long-stemmed lighter. Keep the flame to the charcoal disc until all the edges are glowing and a few sparks have crossed the diameter of the disc.
4. Carefully place the charcoal disc in the censer and sprinkle a layer of the Generic Ritual Blessings incense over the top of the disc.
5. Pick up the bowl of salt. State:

    Creature of salt, element of earth, I call upon your powers to cleanse and neutralize.

6. Sprinkle two pinches of salt into the bowl of water, stating:

   I exorcise thee, o creature of water, that you may cleanse and bless.

7. Set down the bowl of salt, and use your fingers to stir the salt into the water.
8. Take the bowl of water and walk a circle around the altar table. Sprinkle the water as you go, stating:

   By the powers of water and earth, this space is cleansed.

9. Set the water back in its original spot.
10. Light the tea light candle.
11. Pick up the censer and walk the circle again. As you walk the circle, state:

    By air and fire, this space is cleansed and blessed.

12. Stand in the center facing the altar. State:

    By the power of the elements, I am in a sacred space where this rite shall take place.

13. Return the censer to the heat-resistant pad.
14. Light the pillar candle. As you light the pillar candle, invite the spirit you are honoring into the ritual space.

15. Add more incense to the censer. State:

    I offer this incense to you.

16. Take some time and communicate with the spirit of the powder and honor them as you can.

17. When you have finished communicating with the spirit, point your hand toward the ground and walk the circle in reverse. As you walk the circle in reverse, state:

    This space is released. Stay if you wish and go if you must. I thank you for your time.

18. When you are ready to end the ritual, extinguish the incense and the candles. Dispose of the cooled ashes and salt in the trash. Return everything else to its original storage place.

Recharging Your Magical Powder

Feeding the spirit of your powder is only one of the ways that you can help it maintain power over a long period of time. Another technique that allows your powders to store power is the practice of recharging them.

Recharging your powder is much like adding wood to the embers of a campfire. Life and power are still there, but faint. Recharging the powder adds new fuel to it, bringing the powder back to life. When you feed your powders, you only add a small dash of energy. A recharge of a powder brings new energy from four new sources: the four elements.

Through a formal ritual that calls on the four elements, each of the elements will feed the spirit and energetic forces within the powder. Fire reignites life, air provides memory, earth provides strength, and water brings the ability to flow and adapt. When the energy from the elements reaches the forces living in your powder, they are activated and woken up.

As your powder is recharged, a little bit of energy is released to the universe. This energy will empower any spells or workings in process that are using the powder. The remaining energy from the recharge goes into the powder and blends with the old energy to create a refreshed version of the powder's spirit.

When to Recharge Powders

Powders need to be recharged when you feel their power dwindling or when it feels as if the spirit is hibernating. A powder in need of recharge may feel dull, as if all color has been drained and the bare minimum of life exists within. In this case, you can see and feel what is there, but the sensations are not nearly as powerful as when it was freshly created.

Ritual to Recharge Your Magical Powder

Use this ritual to recharge your magical powder. For this exercise, we will recharge the Repelling

Toxic Individuals Powder from chapter 5, "Common Magical Powders."

Be sure to use a taper candle in a color that corresponds to the type of powder you are recharging. The incense used should correspond as well. For best results, perform this ritual monthly.

MATERIALS

- Small table
- Altar cloth
- Mixing bowl
- Taper candle
- Taper candleholder
- Incense
- Censer (with salt or sand in the base to protect against heat damage)
- Small bowl of water
- Small bowl of salt
- Cup of water or shot of alcohol
- Spoon or wand
- Charcoal
- Long-stemmed lighter
- Magical powder
- Shoes and/or wallet

WORKING

1. Set up your work area by placing the altar cloth down first.
2. Place the mixing bowl in the center of the altar. Put the candleholder and candle on one side of the bowl and the incense and censer on the other.

Set the bowl of salt in front of the mixing bowl. Place the cup of water or shot of alcohol behind it. Set the spoon or wand in front of the mixing bowl.

3. Light the candle. State:

   May this candlelight bring life to my magic on this night.

4. Use the tongs to hold the charcoal in one hand. With the other hand, use the long-stemmed lighter to light the charcoal. When the edges of the charcoal are glowing, carefully place the charcoal disc in the censer and sprinkle the incense lightly over the charcoal.

5. Once the smoke from the incense is flowing, state:

   For the power of air and the gift of life.

6. Sit or stand in front of the altar. Call on any of your spirit guides or spirit allies that you work with. If not working with any deities or spirits, state:

   I call upon the powers of the universe to come and aid me in my work this night. May the powers of the elements energize and recharge this magical powder.

7. Pour your magical powder into the mixing bowl.

8. Use your receptive (nondominant) hand to hold the mixing bowl. With your dominant hand, use the spoon or wand to stir the magical powder.

As you stir the powder, recite a chant or mantra based on your intent five to seven times.

9. Hold the bowl safely over the candle. State:

    I call upon the power of fire, that which is the spark of life and fuels all passion. Energize and empower this magical powder. May your warmth and light help manifest (intent for magical powder) with this rite.

10. Pass the bowl through the incense smoke. As you pass the bowl through the smoke, state:

    I call upon the power of air, the mind, and breath of life. Energize and empower this magical powder. May the winds of change help manifest (intent for magical powder) with this rite.

11. Place the small bowl of salt in the mixing bowl. Hold your hands over both bowls. State:

    I call upon the power of earth, that which gives form and strength. May you provide the form which (intent for magical powder) takes in manifestation.

12. Place the bowl of salt back on the altar and grab the bowl of water. Place the bowl of water in the mixing bowl. State:

    I call upon the power of water, power of emotions and transformation. May you take the power of my emotions and help (intent for magical powder) come toward me, flowing freely.

13. Place the bowl of water back on the altar. Return the mixing bowl to the center of the altar. Pick up the glass of water or shot of alcohol. Raise the glass over the altar. State:

    May this drink nourish those spirits which came to empower my magical powder. Thank you for attending this rite.

14. Sprinkle a little of the powder around the candle and censer. State:

    By the power of air and fire, to manifest (type of magical powder) is my desire.

15. Sprinkle a little powder into the bowl of water. State:

    By the power of earth and water, my desire for (type of magical powder) is sent forth.

16. Carefully return the powder to its original storage container.

17. When the powder has returned to its container, pass it through the incense smoke and candle flame one last time.

18. Let the candle and incense burn out completely. Pour the bowl of water down the drain. If you have a permanent altar, set the alcohol or glass of water on the altar to be consumed by spirit, otherwise pour it down the drain as well. Dispose of the cooled candle and incense remains by respectfully placing them in the trash. Clean up and put away the remaining tools.

PART II
Magical Powder Formulas

Common Magical Powders

This selection of powders contains a variety of magical mixtures that can be used to bring things into your life. These magical powders are based on quick results and work as a good general introduction to magical powders. These powders can be added to any spell or ritual, or they can be sprinkled and worked as a spell by themselves.

Block Busting Powders

Block busting powders are used when you need to overcome obstacles in your path. You can use these powders to both create new options and simply remove blocks in your path. The herb abre camino (*Koanophyllon villosum*) is the main powerhouse in block buster work. Other herbs such as basil (*Ocimum basilicum*) and parsley (*Petroselinum crispum*) also work as formidable block busters. Use the following formulas to make powders that will help you overcome blocks and obstacles in your way.

Road Opener Powder

Mix up this Road Opener Powder to create new opportunities for you, or it can simply help you go over and around the obstacles before you to achieve your goals.

MATERIALS

- ¾ cup (180 ml) abre camino (*Koanophyllon villosum*) (to open roads)
- 1½ tablespoons (22 ml) basil (*Ocimum basilicum*) (to open roads, remove blocks)
- 1 tablespoon (15 ml) dill seeds (*Anethum graveolens*) (to attract luck, break hexes)
- 1 tablespoon (15 ml) grains of paradise (*Aframomum melegueta*) (for good luck, removal)
- 1 teaspoon (5 ml) library dirt (to open up opportunities)

Road Opener Mini Packet Spell

This spell works best when you seem to have a never-ending set of blocks in your path to achieving your goals and desires. By calling upon the industrious power of ants, you will always have the energy and power needed to open the roads to your goals.

MATERIALS

- Pen
- Paper
- 2 tablespoons (30 ml) ground dead ants
- 1 tablespoon (15 ml) Road Opener Powder
- Tape

WORKING

1. On the paper, write out what the current blocks in your life are.
2. Sprinkle a tablespoon of ants over the words. State:

    That which was a door blocking my way,
    I have the key to you which unlocks, and
    open shall this door stay.

3. Sprinkle the Road Opener Powder over the words. Repeat the statement from step 2.
4. Use the remaining tablespoon of ground ants to finish covering up the blocks. If more material is needed, continue to add Road Opener Powder until the words are covered.
5. Fold the paper in half away from you. Pound your fist down at the seam to make a tight and secure fold. As you pound your fist over the fold, state:

    Blocks busted away. Forward motions start today.

6. Repeat step 5 until you can no longer fold the packet.

7. Place a piece of tape over the last folded opening to secure the packet.
8. Next time you leave your home, find a trash can far away from where you live and work to toss the packet into. The road to success will now open.

Block Buster Powder

There are times in our lives when the road to success is open but the path is not clear. Use this powder to remove the blocks along the path to your goals.

MATERIALS

- ⅔ cup (160 ml) abre camino (*Koanophyllon villosum*) (to open roads)
- 1 tablespoon (15 ml) basil (*Ocimum basilicum*) (to open roads, remove blocks)
- 1 tablespoon (15 ml) parsley (*Petroselinum crispum*) (to open roads, remove blocks)
- 1 tablespoon (15 ml) rosemary (*Salvia rosmarinus*) (for cleansing, to clean up miscommunication)
- ½ tablespoon (7 ml) sage (*Salvia officinalis*) (for cleansing, removal)

Obstacle Removal Powder

Sometimes the blocks that we need to remove have been caused by baneful magic sent our way. Combine the following ingredients to make a powder that will remove the obstacles in your path without causing the person who hexed you to receive any negative feedback.

MATERIALS

- 1 cup (250 ml) basil (*Ocimum basilicum*) (to open roads, remove blocks)
- 1 tablespoon (15 ml) clover (*Trifolium repens*) (for protection against blocks returning, removal, success)
- 1 tablespoon (15 ml) thyme (*Thymus vulgaris*) (for good luck, purification)
- 1 teaspoon (5 ml) valerian root (*Valeriana officinalis*) (to break curses and hexes)
- 1 tablespoon (15 ml) yarrow (*Achillea millefolium*) (for removal, to break hexes)

Protection from Blocks Charm

Sometimes the blocks we encounter in our lives are the result of baneful magic sent toward us. This spell uses the Obstacle Remover Powder to destroy those blocks and counteract the baneful magic that caused them.

MATERIALS

- Small key chain
- Small plate
- 3 dead beetles (for block busting, protection, removal of barriers)
- Mortar and pestle
- 6 tablespoons (90 ml) Obstacle Removal Powder

WORKING

1. Place your key chain on top of the plate. State:

   Chain that holds a key, open the roads before me.

2. Scatter the dead beetles into the mortar. Use the pestle to pound and grind them into as fine of a powder as you can. While grinding, recite the following chant seven to nine times:

   Beetles that are strong, move those obstacles along. Unlock the doors that are blocked so that forward we may walk.

3. Sprinkle the beetle remains over the key chain, covering it as completely as possible. While scattering the beetle remains, recite the same chant from step 2.

4. Sprinkle the Obstacle Remover Powder over the key chain, covering the key chain and the beetle remains. As you cover the key chain, recite the following chant three to five times:

   All blocks caused by a curse, now be reversed and returned to the earth. With the power neutralized, the curse effectively dies.

5. Leave the key chain on the plate, covered with the beetles and powder, for one week.

6. Once a day for the next week, place your hand on top of the powder mixture and repeat the chant from step 4 three times.

7. After one week, dig the key chain out from the powder pile. Carry it with you and any blocks that you find yourself being faced with can easily be overcome. Carrying this charm breaks the hold the baneful magic had over your life, clearing the blocks and removing the curse at the same time.

Psychic Work & Divination Powders

Divination and psychic work are common practices among witches and magical workers. Learning to trust your intuition can be a difficult process. These powders can be used in spells and rituals to enhance and develop your psychic senses.

Gain Intuition Powder

Mix up this Gain Intuition Powder to call upon the power and wisdom of the snake to help you trust your intuition and discern true messages from trickster spirits or false guidance.

MATERIALS

- 2 large shed snake skins (for insight, mental clarity, wisdom)
- 2 bay leaves (*Laurus nobilis*) (for insight, mental clarity, wisdom)
- 1 tablespoon (15 ml) eyebright leaves (*Euphrasia rostkoviana*) (for insight, mental clarity, mental focus, mental powers, wisdom)

- ½ tablespoon (7 ml) marigold flowers (*Calendula officinalis*) (for intuition, psychic powers, psychic wisdom)
- ½ tablespoon (7 ml) ginkgo leaves (*Ginkgo biloba*) (for insight, mental clarity, mental focus, mental powers, wisdom)

Spirit Wisdom & Insight Spell

The following spell uses the Gain Intuition Powder to help ensure you have clear and accurate communication with your guides when meditating or performing divination.

MATERIALS

- Taper candleholder
- Blue, purple, silver, or white taper candle
- Pin, needle, or knife
- Gain Intuition Powder
- Lighter or matches

WORKING

1. Use the pin, needle, or knife to carve the words "Wisdom" and "Insight" into the candle.
2. Rub the Gain Intuition Powder onto the candle from the bottom to the top, as you are trying to grow and strengthen your intuition.
3. Hold the candle to the center of your forehead and state:

   By this candle's light do I strengthen my spiritual insight.

4. Set the candle into the candleholder and light the candle.
5. Burn the candle for ten to fifteen minutes. As the candle burns, know that your psychic senses will grow stronger.
6. After ten to fifteen minutes, extinguish the candle and let it cool.
7. Once a day until the candle has completely burned, repeat steps 6 and 7.
8. When the candle has burned down, you can dispose of the remains.

Divination Blessing Powder

Connecting with your tool is one of the first things that should be done upon receiving or purchasing a new divination tool. Combine these ingredients to make Divination Blessing Powder. Burying your tool in this powder and dusting the bag or container your tool will be stored in with it will provide a psychic charge that will help you have clear and accurate readings.

Materials

- ½ cup (125 ml) mugwort (*Artemisia vulgaris*) (for divination, psychic abilities)
- 2 tablespoons (30 ml) lemongrass (*Cymbopogon citratus*) (for psychic powers)
- 1½ tablespoons (22 ml) anise seed (*Illicium verum*) (for divination)

- ½ tablespoon (7 ml) mullein (*Verbascum thapsus*) (for divination)

Psychic Dreams Powder

Psychic Dreams Powder can be worked as a way to start using your dreams to engage with spirit and your psychic senses. When using this powder, it becomes easier to receive messages from spirit and your intuition in your dreams.

Materials

- ¾ cup (180 ml) marigold (*Calendula officinalis*) (for psychic dreams)
- 1 tablespoon (15 ml) anise seeds (*Illicium verum*) (for psychic dreams)
- 1 tablespoon (15 ml) celery seeds (*Apium graveolens*) (for mental clarity, psychic dreams)
- 1 tablespoon (15 ml) eyebright (*Euphrasia rostkoviana*) (for psychic sight)
- 1 tablespoon (15 ml) jasmine (*Jasminum grandiflorum*) (for prophetic dreams)

Mini Plushie Psychic Power Charm

Stuffed animals and plushies come in many different sizes, from small and hand sized to large and requiring both arms to hold. This spell uses the Psychic Dreams Powder to create a charm that you can keep by your bedside to receive psychic dreams. Small beanbag plushies are ideal for this work.

MATERIALS

- Scissors
- Plushie
- Psychic Dreams Powder
- Thread that matches the plushie's color
- Needle

WORKING

1. Use the scissors to cut along one of the back seams of the plushie.
2. Pull out most of the stuffing and set it aside.
3. Begin to fill the plushie back up—this time with the stuffing and the Psychic Dreams Powder. Combine both materials as you work.
4. When the plushie has been filled, thread the needle and stitch the seam closed. Do your best to sew it as tight as possible.
5. Place the plushie on your pillow and keep it there. The longer you keep the plushie on your pillow, the higher your chance for psychic dreams.

Spirit Work Powders

The following powders can be used to create charms and talismans to help you connect with your spirit guides and allies. Each charm allows you to contact the spirit represented with more ease and provides a way to always keep the spirit's blessings and energy with you.

Angelic Aid Powder

Angels are a wonderful type of spirit to work with. Angelic forces were the first spirits I worked with during my journey as a witch. I have used this powder to work with both the angels of Christianity and the general occult spirits known as angels. This powder can also be burned as an incense and used as an offering to angelic spirits.

MATERIALS

- ½ cup (125 ml) angelica root (*Angelica archangelica*) (for angelic forces)
- 2½ tablespoons (37 ml) frankincense (*Boswellia sacra*) (for angels, power, protection)
- 1½ tablespoons (22 ml) copal (*Bursera odorata*) (for angelic blessings, protection, spirituality)
- 1½ tablespoons (22 ml) myrrh (*Commiphora myrrha*) (for angels, power, protection)
- ½ tablespoon (7 ml) rosemary (*Salvia rosmarinus*) (for angels, to attract spirits)

Dragon Power Powder

Mix up and use this powder to call upon the power and strength of dragon spirits. The powder works best when you already have a relationship with a dragon spirit.

MATERIALS

- 1 cup (250 ml) powdered dragon's blood (*Dracaena cinnabari*) (for dragon power)

- 1½ tablespoons (22 ml) watercress (*Nasturtium officinale*) (for dragon power)
- 1 tablespoon (15 ml) rosemary (*Salvia rosmarinus*) (for blessings, dragon power, spirit energy, dragon power, to attract spirits)
- ½ tablespoon (7 ml) basil (*Ocimum basilicum*) (for dragon power and spirits, spiritual power)
- Dead dragonfly (for dragon spirits)

Draconic Protection Charm

This spell provides you with the protection and power of a dragon spirit. By working this spell, you ensure that no one will mess with you without dealing with dragon fury.

MATERIALS

- Dragon figure small enough to hold in one hand
- Small plate
- Dragon Power Powder

WORKING

1. Place the dragon figure on the plate.
2. Sprinkle the Dragon Power Powder over and around the dragon figure. While sprinkling the powder, recite the following chant until the powder is gone:

   Dragon spirits, I ask of you to provide me protection that is new.

3. Leave the figure on the plate, covered and surrounded by the powder, for twenty-four hours.

After twenty-four hours, clean off and dispose of the powder in the trash. The figure is now charged with dragon spirit power.

4. Place the figure somewhere in your home to watch over the inhabitants and protect the home. Repeat once a month to keep the charm charged.

Ancestor Blessings Powder

Use this powder when you want to call on your ancestors in your magical work. While creating this powder, recite any prayers you say to honor your ancestors. Those prayers, along with the materials, will channel the energy of your ancestors into your work.

MATERIALS

- ½ cup (125 ml) basil (*Ocimum basilicum*) (for blessing, ancestors, underworld work)
- 1½ tablespoons (22 ml) black-eyed Susan flowers (*Rudbeckia hirta*) (for connection with the dead)
- 1 tablespoon (15 ml) frankincense (*Boswellia sacra*) (for blessing, cleansing, to attract spirits)
- 1 tablespoon (15 ml) parsley (*Petroselinum crispum*) (for ancestors, the dead, underworld work)
- ½ tablespoon (7 ml) myrrh (*Commiphora myrrha*) (for blessing, cleansing, to attract spirits)

Ancestral Protection Charm

The following ritual calls upon the power of your ancestors to protect you in your day-to-day life.

MATERIALS

- Mini bottle with cork to seal
- Small fingernail clipping of yours
- Ancestor Blessings Powder

WORKING

1. Open the mini bottle and place your fingernail clipping inside. As you place the clipping inside, state:

   To surround me with your protection.

2. Fill the bottle with the Ancestor Blessings Powder, covering and surrounding the fingernail clipping with the powder.
3. Seal the mini bottle with its cork. Shake the bottle and state:

   Blessed ancestors, I call upon you to bless me with protection that is true. I call upon your protection today; repel that which causes harm. Send it far away.

4. Either carry the bottle with you for protection or place the bottle somewhere in your home for your ancestors to protect your household.

Mental Health Powders

The first area of magic that I engaged in was that of healing magic. The healing work I specialized in dealt with maintaining my mental health. These powders help manage the various symptoms of mental health issues, including anxiety, depression, and flashbacks. These mixtures can also help you process and express difficult emotions.

Anxiety Relief Powder

Use this powder in spells that are performed to help relieve feelings of anxiety. This powder will not replace anxiety medications or fix anxiety disorders; it is simply a magical tool to help you deal with anxiety so that your best health may manifest. This powder also makes an excellent incense.

MATERIALS

- ½ cup (125 ml) lavender (*Lavandula officinalis*) (for anxiety relief, peace)
- 2 tablespoons (30 ml) chamomile (*Matricaria recutita*) (for anxiety relief, peace)
- 1 tablespoon (15 ml) peppermint (*Mentha piperita*) (for anxiety relief, peace)
- ½ tablespoon (7 ml) catnip (*Nepeta cataria*) (for anxiety relief, happiness, peace)
- ½ tablespoon (7 ml) lemon balm (*Melissa officinalis*) (for anxiety relief, peace)

Anxiety Relief Spell

Use this spell to help release any anxieties you are experiencing. As with any healing spell, this spell is not a replacement for professional care or any medication. This spell will simply help manage the anxiety so that you can deal with the situation, heal, and move forward.

MATERIALS

- Purple or blue taper candle
- Pin, needle, or knife
- Anxiety Relief Powder
- Taper candleholder
- Lighter or matches

WORKING

1. Take the taper candle in your hand. As you hold the candle, focus on your anxieties and stressors and direct them into the candle.
2. Use the pin, needle, or knife to carve the words "Anxiety Relief" on two sides of the candle.
3. Rub the Anxiety Relief Powder over the candle.
4. Set the candle in the candleholder.
5. Light the candle. As you do so, state:

   Candle that I light today, burn this anxiety away.

6. Burn the candle for ten to fifteen minutes. As the candle burns, your anxieties will be released into the universe, freeing you from their weight.
7. After ten to fifteen minutes, extinguish the candle and let it cool.
8. Repeat steps 6 and 7 once a day until the candle has completely burned.
9. Once the candle has burned down, dispose of the remains in the trash. Repeat the spell as needed.

Depression Relief Powder

Use this powder in spells that deal with healing depression. This powder will not cure depression but can be used to help manage symptoms. Managing your symptoms will allow you to live a more fulfilled life.

MATERIALS

- 6 tablespoons (90 ml) chamomile flowers (*Matricaria recutita*) (for depression relief, happiness, peace)
- 2½ tablespoons (37 ml) lavender (*Lavandula officinalis*) (for depression relief)
- 1 tablespoon (15 ml) lemon balm (*Melissa officinalis*) (for depression relief, healing)
- 1 tablespoon (15 ml) rosemary (*Salvia rosmarinus*) (for depression relief, healing)
- ½ tablespoon (7 ml) Saint-John's-wort (*Hypericum perforatum*) (for depression relief, healing)

Happiness Powder

This powder can be used to bring happiness and joy into your life. It can be used as an attraction powder as well as a healing powder when dealing with some mental illnesses, such as post-traumatic stress disorder, depression, and anxiety.

MATERIALS

- ½ cup (125 ml) marjoram (*Origanum majorana*) (to attract happiness and joy)
- 1½ tablespoon (22 ml) catnip (*Nepeta cataria*) (for friendship, happiness, joy)
- 1 tablespoon (15 ml) pink rose petals (*Rosa rubiginosa*) (for happiness, joy, love)

Attract Joy, Peace & Happiness Working

This spell uses Happiness Powder to bring joy, light, and happiness into your life as a brief reprieve from anxiety or depression. One day of joy and light can help you feel stronger, allowing you to deal with some of the harder issues in your life.

MATERIALS

- Pen
- Paper
- Happiness Powder
- Taper candleholder
- Pin, needle, or knife
- Blue taper candle

- Lavender (*Lavandula officinalis*) essential oil (for healing, peace)
- Lighter or matches

WORKING

1. In the center of the paper, write out your name, date of birth, and wish to bring happiness and joy into your life.
2. Cover your name, date of birth, and intent with the Happiness Powder. Set the remaining powder to the side.
3. Fold the paper in half toward you three or four times. Set the folded paper underneath the candleholder.
4. Use the pin, needle, or knife to carve the word "Happiness" on one side of the taper candle. On the other side, carve the words "Joy" and "Peace."
5. Anoint the candle with the lavender essential oil from the center out to the top and then from the center to the bottom.
6. Rub the remaining Happiness Powder into the candle where you carved the words.
7. Set the candle in the holder and light the candle. As you light the candle, state:

   Candle that is burning bright, light the way for happiness, joy, and delight.

8. Burn the candle for five minutes a day.

9. After five minutes, extinguish the candle and let it cool.
10. Repeat steps 7, 8, and 9 once a day until the candle has burned completely.
11. Once the candle has burned down, dispose of the remains in the trash.

Legal & Law-Related Powders

Dealing with legal issues is never an easy thing to do. These powders are here to help you get the outcome you desire. Whether you are experiencing divorce issues or dealing with a vindictive neighbor, these magical powders will boost your chances of success in the legal world. Note that using these powders is not a substitute for receiving advice from a legal professional.

When Dealing with Court Cases Powder

Mix and use this powder in spells and workings that deal with the court and legal issues. This powder helps increase the odds that the outcome will be in your favor.

MATERIALS

- 6 tablespoons (90 ml) galangal root (*Alpinia galanga*) (for justice)
- 2 tablespoons (30 ml) dill (*Anethum graveolens*) (to keep law away)

- 1½ tablespoon (22 ml) devil's shoestring (*Viburnum alnifolium*) (to keep law away)
- ½ tablespoon (7 ml) rosemary (*Salvia rosmarinus*) (for communication, to open minds)
- 1 teaspoon (5 ml) courtyard dirt (for legal issues, power of location)

Strength & Courage Powder

Use this powder when you need to increase your inner strength and face difficult situations. When it comes to dealing with the court, justice system, and law, this powder can help bring out the resolve to handle the situation and all people involved.

MATERIALS

- ½ cup (125 ml) thyme (*Thymus vulgaris*) (for protection, strength)
- 1½ tablespoon (22 ml) plantain (*Plantago major*) (for resilience, strength)
- 1 tablespoon (15 ml) angelica root (*Angelica archangelica*) (for protection, strength)
- 1 tablespoon (15 ml) woodruff (*Galium odoratum*) (for control of the situation, courage, protection)
- ½ tablespoon (7 ml) pennyroyal (*Mentha pulegium*) (for peace, protection, strength)

Strength & Courage Charm

There are times when we need a boost of courage to get things done, such as leaving an abusive relationship or starting the process of getting a divorce.

This spell uses the Strength and Courage Powder to create a charm that will give you a boost of courage and strength.

If you cannot find a shield penny, that's okay. Any penny can work, as copper has protective energy.

MATERIALS

- Small metal tin
- Shield penny
- Acorn top (*Quercus* spp.) (for courage, strength)
- Strength and Courage Powder
- Fresh sprig or ½ tablespoon (7 ml) rosemary (*Salvia rosmarinus*) (for clarity of thought)
- Cat claw sheaths (for protection, strength)

WORKING

1. Open the tin and place the penny inside. State:

   From this shield, my inner strength I shall yield.

2. Set the acorn top in the tin. State:

   Like the oak tall and strong, I have the power to move along.

3. Place the rosemary in the tin. State:

   As I gather my courage this time, I have rosemary for clarity of mind.

4. Sprinkle the Strength and Courage Powder over the materials in the tin.

5. Seal the tin.

6. Shake the tin vigorously. As you shake the tin, recite the following statement seven times:

   Inner strength for me, to face this problem freely.

7. Carry the charm with you when you are dealing with the issue you are trying to face. If you must talk to an individual or group of people, repeat step 6 before starting the conversation.
8. When the situation has resolved, open the tin and dispose of the contents in a trash can away from your home. Wash and cleanse the tin and use it in future magical works.

Hear My Truth Powder

Use this powder when you need to get your side of the story heard. It works best when incorporated in sachets or other charms.

MATERIALS

- 6 tablespoons (90 ml) galangal root (*Alpinia galanga*) (for justice, protection)
- 1½ tablespoons (22 ml) rosemary (*Salvia rosmarinus*) (for communication, to encourage others to listen, open minds)
- 1 tablespoon (15 ml) lavender (*Lavandula officinalis*) (to cool reactions, open minds, sweeten)
- ½ tablespoon (7 ml) masterwort (*Astrantia major*) (to influence target [slight control])
- 1 teaspoon (5 ml) court dirt (for power of the court)

Hear My Plea—Court Assistance Spell

When dealing with the court, it is essential to make sure that all sides of the story or situation are taken into consideration. This spell works with the Hear My Truth Powder to ensure that your version of the story is heard.

MATERIALS

- Paper
- Pen
- Fresh spring or 1 tablespoon (15 ml) rosemary (*Salvia rosmarinus*) (to open minds)
- ½ tablespoon (7 ml) sugar (*Saccharum officinarum*) (for sweetening, to open others to your view)
- 1 tablespoon (15 ml) Hear My Truth Powder

WORKING

1. On the paper, write out your petition to have your side of the story heard and understood. Include all essential details. Under your petition, write what it is you want to get out of the situation.
2. Set the rosemary on the petition paper. As you place the rosemary, state:

   Herb of the mind, have them hear my tale this time.

3. Cover the rosemary with the sugar. State:

   Sugar that is sweet, my desires shall they meet.

4. Cover the rosemary and sugar with the Hear My Truth Powder. As you sprinkle the powder over the rosemary and sugar, state:

   Hear my truth on this day. Open your mind to what I have to say.

5. Fold the piece of paper two or three times toward you. Keep as much of the sugar, herbs, and powder inside of the paper as you can.
6. Carry the folded charm with you when you go to court and the case is being argued.
7. When the case is over, toss the charm in a trash can in the courthouse. This will ensure that the justice served will last.

Love & Lust Powders

Love comes in many forms. Love powders work to both attract new love into your life and to enhance feelings of love that are already present in your life. From self-love to romantic love and friendship and to animal love, love powders can help bring whatever love you need into your life.

Romantic Love Powder

Use this powder in spells to attract romantic love into your life. For best results, I recommend using this mix as a daily dusting body powder.

MATERIALS

- ¾ cup (180 ml) red rose petals (*Rosa rubiginosa*) (for love)
- 1½ tablespoons (22 ml) cardamom (*Elettaria cardamomum*) (for love, lust)
- 1 tablespoon (15 ml) lemon zest (*Citrus limon*) (for love)
- ½ tablespoon (7 ml) yellow dock (*Rumex crispus*) (to attract love)
- 1 teaspoon (5 ml) cinnamon (*Cinnamomum verum*) (for desire, love, lust, passion)

Love Come to Me Spell

The best way to find love in your life is to simply live and experience your life. This spell uses Romantic Love Powder to bring love to you as you simply go about and enjoy your day-to-day life.

MATERIALS

- Bowl
- Spoon or wand
- ½ cup (125 ml) Romantic Love Powder
- 1 cup (250 ml) baby powder
- Small jar with a lid
- Makeup brush

WORKING

1. In the bowl, mix the Romantic Love Powder and the baby powder together. As you mix the materials in the bowl, recite the following mantra five times:

True love comes to me. A love that comes naturally and freely.

2. Once the materials are mixed thoroughly, use the spoon or wand to move the powder from the bowl to the jar. Seal the jar.
3. Whenever you go out for the night or to socialize, use the makeup brush to dust the powder in your shoes. Every step you take will activate the power within the powder and bring love into your life.
4. Continue to apply the powder to your shoes when you go out until you find yourself in the type of relationship you want to be in.
5. Once the relationship has developed, dispose of any remaining powder in the trash. Maintain the relationship through your regular mundane methods.

Lover's Lust Powder

Some people don't want romantic relationships. They just want someone to care about and occasionally have sex with. This powder will help you attract that sort of lust-with-love relationship.

MATERIALS

- ½ cup (125 ml) celery seed (*Apium graveolens*) (for desire, love, lust, passion)
- 2 tablespoons (30 ml) red rose leaves (*Rosa rubiginosa*) (for love, passion)

- 1 tablespoon (15 ml) damiana leaves (*Turnera diffusa*) (for desire, lust, passion, sexuality)
- ½ tablespoon (7 ml) ginseng (*Panax ginseng*) (for fire, desire, lust)
- ½ tablespoon (7 ml) orange zest (*Citrus sinensis*) (for love, sexuality)

Gentle Self-Love Powder

When we love ourselves, it is easier to attract love into our lives. This gentle powder is designed to help you love yourself so that love of all kinds can be in your life.

MATERIALS

- ½ cup (125 ml) baby powder
- 1½ tablespoons (22 ml) pink rose petals (*Rosa rubiginosa*) (for friendship, kindness, love, self-esteem)
- 1½ tablespoons (22 ml) catnip (*Nepeta cataria*) (for friendship, happiness)
- ½ tablespoon (7 ml) jasmine (*Jasminum grandiflorum*) (for love)
- ½ tablespoon (7 ml) lavender (*Lavandula officinalis*) (for love, peace)

Self-Esteem Boost Spell

This spell uses Gentle Self-Love Powder to give yourself a boost in self-esteem.

MATERIALS

- Pink chime candle
- Olive oil or a love oil
- Chime candleholder
- Mortar and pestle
- Butterfly wings or shed chrysalis (for beauty, renewal, self-love)
- Gentle Self-Love Powder
- Spoon or wand
- Small jar with lid
- Pen
- Label sticker
- Makeup brush

WORKING

1. Anoint the chime candle with oil. Rub the oil on the candle either from the center out or from the bottom to the top.

2. Set the chime candle in the candleholder.

3. Place the butterfly wings or chrysalis in the mortar.

4. Sprinkle the Gentle Self-Love Powder in the mortar, and use the pestle to grind the materials into one cohesive powder.

5. Transfer the powder from the mortar and pestle to the jar. Label it "Self-Love Powder."

6. Whenever you feel self-conscious, take the makeup brush and dip it into the powder. Brush the powder over your feet, wrists,

and across your chest. This will give you a boost of self-esteem and alleviate your feelings of self-consciousness.

Luck & Money Powders

These powders can be used when you need to boost your luck. In some cases, luck is seen as blessings from God or the spirits. Other times luck is simply considered great chances. These powders work to bring luck to you, regardless of the source.

Luck and money often go hand in hand. The money powders in this section are for workings when you are trying to increase your finances. These powders are also great for sales and service-based businesses, as they can bring in more customers.

LUCK REFRESHER POWDER

Every once and a while, our good luck runs out or becomes stale. Use this powder when you feel you've had some bad luck or need a batch of fresh good luck.

MATERIALS

- ¾ cup (180 ml) dill leaves or seeds (*Anethum graveolens*) (for good luck, success)
- 1 tablespoon (15 ml) coriander leaves or seeds (*Coriandrum sativum*) (for good luck)

- 1 tablespoon (15 ml) grains of paradise (*Aframomum melegueta*) (for luck)
- ½ tablespoon (7 ml) cramp bark (*Viburnum opulus*) (for good luck)
- ½ tablespoon (7 ml) gravel root (*Eutrochium purpureum*) (for good luck)

Lucky Locket Charm

Wear this locket charm to bring good luck into your life. You can also give this locket to someone you feel needs a boost in their luck.

MATERIALS

- Small slip of paper
- Pen
- Locket and chain
- Luck Refresher Powder

WORKING

1. On the slip of paper, write the words "Lucky Locket." Fold the slip of paper in half.
2. Open the locket and sprinkle a pinch of the Luck Refresher Powder into the bottom. State:

    Good luck that is sweet. All good things I now greet.

3. Place the paper on top of the powder. State:

    This lucky locket I do make, paving the way for things that are great.

4. Cover the paper with the remaining Luck Refresher Powder and close the locket.
5. Wear the locket daily to attract good luck into your life. Keep wearing the locket for as long as you need extra luck.

Money Draw Powder

Use this powder to draw money into your life. It works best when sprinkled over cash or coins kept in your wallet or purse.

MATERIALS

- ¾ cup (180 ml) magnetic sand (for attraction)
- 1½ tablespoons (22 ml) yarrow flowers (*Achillea millefolium*) (to draw money)
- 1 tablespoon(15 ml) cinnamon powder (*Cinnamomum verum*) (for money)
- ½ tablespoon(7 ml) sunflower seeds (*Helianthus annuus*) (for money, prosperity)
- 1 teaspoon (5 ml) bank dirt (for money)

Successful Sales Powder

This powder works specifically for sales. From direct sales to retail and services, sales allow businesses to succeed. Use this powder in spells to attract sales for your business.

MATERIALS

- ¾ cup (180 ml) ginger (*Zingiber officinale*) (for money, success)

- 1½ tablespoons (22 ml) alfalfa (*Medicago sativa*) (for fast money, money, prosperity)
- 1 tablespoon (15 ml) goldenrod (*Solidago altissima*) (for money)
- 1 tablespoon (15 ml) yellow dock (*Rumex crispus*) (for money, to attract sales)
- ½ tablespoon (7 ml) pine needles (*Pinus* spp.) (for fertility, money, prosperity, success)

Successful Sales Charm

Sometimes customers are difficult. This spell uses Successful Sales Powder to ensure that sales interactions with testy customers go better, and in your favor.

Materials

- 2 business cards belonging to you or the business (Slips of paper with the business name written on them work as a substitute.)
- Slip of paper
- Pen
- Sugar (*Saccharum officinarum*) (to sweeten people)
- Masterwort (*Astrantia major*) (to influence others)
- Successful Sales Powder
- Green ribbon or thread
- Scissors

Working

1. Place one of the business cards face down so the back is facing you.

2. On the slip of paper, write a simple petition for difficult customers to actively listen to what you have to say.
3. Place the slip of paper onto the business card with the petition facing up.
4. Sprinkle the sugar over the petition. State:

   May this sweeten their personality, and may it sweeten them up to me.

5. Place the masterwort over the sugar. State:

   Masterwort to influence those who are difficult and cause them to have common sense.

6. Cover the masterwort with the Successful Sales Powder. State:

   Successful sales on this day come this way. Success and prosperity here shall stay.

7. Set the other business card on top of the herbs and powders. This card should be face up.
8. Carefully pick up the pile with one hand. Use your other hand to begin wrapping the green ribbon or thread around the bundle as best you can. Your goal is to secure the pile into a sort of package. As you wrap the ribbon or thread around the bundle, recite the following chant until it is covered:

   Successful sales on this day come this way. Success and prosperity are here to stay.

9. When you feel that the packet is covered, tie a tight knot in the ribbon or thread around it. As you make the knot, state:

    This packet is now sealed. May the magic within be revealed.

10. Bring the packet to work with you. When you engage with the customer, play with the packet. Know that as you speak to them, the spell is being released and the energy is being sent to manifest.
11. Keep the packet for use with all difficult customers. When you feel that the charm has done its work, use scissors to cut open the bundle and toss the materials in the trash.

Protection Powders

Protection magic is one of the most basic forms of magical work. The following powders repel or redirect evil and negative energy in order to protect against them.

Repelling Toxic Individuals Powder

Keeping toxic people out of your life can be a difficult task. Use this powder to keep those unwanted individuals away from your friends and family. For best results, scatter this powder around the home or sprinkle it in your shoes.

MATERIALS

- ¾ cup (180 ml) marjoram (*Origanum majorana*) (to drive off forces that would harm your family)
- 1½ tablespoons (22 ml) hyssop (*Hyssopus officinalis*) (for removal, to neutralize energy, repel negativity)
- 1 tablespoon (15 ml) mace (*Myristica fragrans*) (for removal, to repel evil)
- 1 tablespoon (15 ml) white mustard seeds (*Brassica hirta*) (to repel evil)
- ½ tablespoon (7 ml) cumin seeds (*Cuminum cyminum*) (for reflection, reversal, to deflect evil, repel baneful energy)

Evil Eye Protection Powder

The evil eye is one of the most common curses in the world. Use this powder to protect against and remove the evil eye. This powder works best when accompanied by a candle cleansing spell.

MATERIALS

- ½ cup (125 ml) cat's eye shells (for protection against the evil eye)
- 1½ tablespoons (22 ml) lilac flowers (*Syringa vulgaris*) (for protection against baneful magic)
- 1 tablespoon (15 ml) pine needles (*Pinus* spp.) (for cleansing, protection, removal)
- 1 tablespoon (15 ml) sage (*Salvia officinalis*) (for cleansing, protection against the evil eye, removal)
- ½ tablespoon (7 ml) lemon balm (*Melissa officinalis*) (for cleansing, hex breaking, protection, removal)

Evil Eye Candle Cleansing Spell

Many cultures have their own spells and workings to remove and protect against the evil eye. This spell is my own variation on a candle cleansing spell. The working uses Evil Eye Protection Powder as well as a candle to remove the evil eye.

This spell can be done for oneself or someone else. If performing this working for yourself, simply rub the candle over your body instead.

MATERIALS

- White taper candle
- Olive oil or a charged anointing oil (for cleansing, removal, or reversal)
- Evil Eye Protection Powder
- Taper candleholder
- Lighter or matches

WORKING

1. Run the taper candle over the body of the individual with the evil eye upon them. Start at their head and move down to their feet, being careful not to wipe back over an area just rubbed.
2. Once their body has been rubbed down with the candle, anoint the candle with oil from top to bottom.
3. Rub Evil Eye Protection Powder over the candle from bottom to top. As you rub the powder over the candle, state:

Evil eye cast upon me, from your curse I am free.

4. Set the candle in the candleholder and light the candle. State:

    By this candlelight, the evil eye shall take flight.

5. Let the candle burn for ten to fifteen minutes.
6. After ten to fifteen minutes, extinguish the candle and let it cool.
7. Once a day, repeat steps 4, 5, and 6 until the candle has completely burned out. When the candle has burned down, toss the remains in a trash can away from your home. This will finalize the removal of the evil eye.

Invisibility Powder

Sometimes in our lives there are moments when we do not wish to be noticed when out in public. This powder works as a glamour to keep us hidden in plain sight. Sprinkle the powder in your shoes or carry it in a charm to achieve best results.

MATERIALS

- ½ cup (125 ml) marjoram (*Origanum majorana*) (to repel unwanted attention)
- 2 tablespoons (30 ml) stinging nettle (*Urtica dioica*) (for protection, reversal, to repel attention)
- 1 tablespoon (15 ml) ivy (*Hedera helix*) (for camouflage, to hide)

- ½ tablespoon (7 ml) alum (for protection)
- ½ tablespoon (7 ml) wolf or snake tracks (You can use shed fur or skin as a substitute.) (for invisibility)

Out of Sight Invisibility Charm

Use this spell when you just want to be left alone while out in public. Work with Invisibility Powder to create a glamour and illusion of being invisible.

MATERIALS

- Personal effect, such as a piece of hair or fingernail (A photo of yourself or slip of paper with your name and date of birth on it works as a substitute.)
- Small bottle with lid (Empty pill containers work well for this.)
- Invisibility Powder
- 2 to 3 mirror or glass fragments (for reflection)

WORKING

1. Place your personal effect in the bottle. State:

   To protect myself, I hide a part of myself.

2. Cover the personal effect with the Invisibility Powder. As you cover the personal effect, state:

   Powder of invisibility, hidden in plain sight I shall be.

3. Add the mirror or glass fragments to the bottle, stating:

   Reflect away attention from me to grant me invisibility.

4. Seal the bottle with the lid.
5. Shake the bottle to mix the ingredients together. As you shake the bottle, see yourself slipping through the crowds unseen, overlooked by everyone. Direct the energy from those thoughts and images into the bottle.
6. Carry the charm with you when you next travel and wish to be unseen. Anytime you feel that someone may be taking an interest in you, give the bottle a shake to activate its magical charge.
7. Dispose of the materials in the trash when the charm is no longer needed, saving the bottle for future spellwork.

Wishing Powders

Wish granting is one of the most universal forms of magic. Wish powder can be used in any spell to provide the magic of a wish as a boost for the working, or it can be used by itself as a form of spellwork.

Penta Power Wish Powder

This powder uses the power of five curios associated with wishing. This powder works best when accompanied by candle magic.

MATERIALS

- ½ cup (125 ml) dandelion seed heads, leaves, or root (*Taraxacum officinale*) (for wishes)

- 2½ tablespoons (37 ml) bay leaves (*Laurus nobilis*) (for wishes)
- 1 tablespoon (15 ml) magnetic sand (for attraction, manifestation, wishes)
- ½ tablespoon (7 ml) ginseng root (*Panax ginseng*) (to grant wishes)
- ½ teaspoon (2.5 ml) crossroads dirt (for power, wishes, to send energy in the four cardinal directions)

Five Candles, Five Wishes Spell

This spell uses Penta Power Wish Powder to grant the spell caster five wishes.

MATERIALS

- 5 chime candleholders
- Five slips of paper
- Pen
- 5 white chime candles
- Penta Power Wish Powder
- Lighter or matches

WORKING

1. Set the chime candleholders out so they make the shape a pentagon with the top point facing you.
2. On each slip of paper, write out one of your wishes. Set each slip of paper in front of one of the chime candleholders.
3. Place one candle in each candleholder.

4. Read each wish aloud and then fold up the paper, setting the paper under the candleholder.
5. Sprinkle the Penta Power Wish Powder around each of the chime candleholders. As you sprinkle the powder, state:

   I cast this wish with all my might, that its manifestation is now in sight.

6. Light each candle. As you do so, state:

   By this candle's fire and light does my desire manifest from this rite.

7. Let the candles burn out completely.
8. Once the candles have burned down, dispose of the candle remains and powder in a trash can near your home. Dispose of each slip in a different trash can to spread the magic out, creating more avenues for your wishes to manifest.

Natural Wish Powder

This wish powder evokes the power of the element of earth and nature. Use this in any spell or working to add the foundation of a strong wish to the magic at hand. Toss this powder into the wind for best results.

MATERIALS

- ¾ cup (180 ml) dandelion root (*Taraxacum officinale*) (for making wishes)
- 1½ tablespoons (22 ml) bay leaves (*Laurus nobilis*) (for wishes)

- 1 tablespoon (15 ml) powdered dragon's blood (*Dracaena cinnabari*) (for dragon energy, power, magic, wishes)
- ½ tablespoon (7 ml) anise seed (*Illicium verum*) (for magic, to grant wishes)
- ½ teaspoon (2.5 ml) crossroads dirt (for magic, power, to grant wishes, send energy in the four cardinal directions)

Spicy Wish Powder

This powder is powered by herbs that are hot and used to spice things up. Use this powder when you need a wish granted fast.

MATERIALS

- ½ cup (125 ml) grains of paradise (*Aframomum melegueta*) (to grant wishes)
- 1½ tablespoons (22 ml) ginseng root (*Panax ginseng*) (to grant wishes)
- 1 tablespoon (15 ml) bay leaves (*Laurus nobilis*) (for wishes)
- ½ tablespoon (7 ml) rosemary (*Salvia rosmarinus*) (as a spiritual aid to manifest wishes)
- ½ teaspoon (2.5 ml) cayenne pepper (*Capsicum annuum*) (for fire, power, speed)

Gingerroot Wish Charm

Gingerroot is a powerful herb when it comes to granting wishes. The following charm uses the power of the fire of ginger and the Spicy Wish Powder to grant your wish.

MATERIALS

- Gingerroot (*Zingiber officinale*) (to grant wishes)
- Pin, needle, or knife
- Olive oil or another anointing oil
- Spicy Wish Powder

WORKING

1. Hold the gingerroot in one hand. With the other hand, carefully use the pin, needle, or knife to carve the word "Wish" into two sides of the gingerroot.
2. Anoint the gingerroot with the olive oil.
3. Rub the gingerroot with the Spicy Wish Powder. As you rub the root with the powder, state your wish.
4. Set the gingerroot somewhere it can dry.
5. Once the gingerroot has dried, carry it with you for the day, thinking about your wish.
6. At the end of the day, bury the gingerroot outside. As you bury the root, state:

   Gingerroot, I ask of thee to manifest my wish for me. I wish (state your wish).

7. Walk away and let the root send your wish into the earth.

Witches' Salts

As a base powder, salt absorbs and neutralizes any negativity sent toward you and the work you are doing. When salt neutralizes the negativity and problems directed toward you and your goal, the herbs and other materials in the spell can fully work to bring your intent into manifestation.

Salts as magical powders are probably my favorite. Note, however, that covering some materials with salt can cause them to be corroded and damaged. This is why salt is typically cleaned up within twenty-four hours. Witches' salts work best as a filling for a charm or with candles.

A word of warning before going forward: Salts such as Himalayan pink salt and black Hawaiian salt are sold on the market for use in cooking and other dietary needs.

These are not the salts referred to when someone mentions witches' black salt or red salt. Witches' colored salts are not to be ingested or confused with culinary salts with similar names.

Black Salt

Black salt is the most famous and well known of all witches' salts. This salt has a history of being misunderstood and misapplied. Black salt originated as a form of protection magic—specifically protection magic against witchcraft. Today, black salt is used to protect against baneful magic and to occasionally reverse baneful magic to its source.

The creation of black salt is one of the reasons many witches keep the ashes from any magical workings they do. When materials are burned, they create ash. Ash has magical properties of protection and neutralization. When added to salt, you get a potent powder that absorbs and neutralizes the energy sent at you, protecting you from baneful forces.

Black Witches' Salt #1

This black salt is your most basic black salt. Use it for protection and removal magic. Add it to witches' jars and other charms to boost your protection.

MATERIALS

- ½ cup (125 ml) sea salt (for absorption, neutralization)
- 3 tablespoons (45 ml) ground charcoal (for protection, to neutralize)
- 1 tablespoon (15 ml) ash (for absorption, neutralization)

Mini Witches' Jar Necklace Charm

This mini spell jar works as a wonderful charm that you can wear or carry with you. Mini charm bottles are available for sale year-round at many craft stores.

MATERIALS

- Mini glass jar necklace charm large enough to hold 2 pins or needles
- Personal effect (A small lock of hair or fingernail clipping is recommended.)
- 2 pins or needles
- Black Witches' Salt #1
- 18-to-24-inch (30-to-46-cm) necklace chain

WORKING

1. Open the mini jar and place your personal effect inside. As you add it, state:

   Effect of mine, a decoy shall you be. All attacks reach you instead of me.

2. Add the pins or needles to the jar. State:

   To attack and destroy all that is sent this way.

3. Fill the jar with the witches' salt. You want to cover the pins or needles and your personal effect with the salt.
4. Seal the jar and attach it to the chain. Wear the necklace daily to protect yourself against any ill will or baneful magic that may be sent your way.

Black Witches' Salt #2

This black salt is perfect for return-to-sender work. The galangal root (*Alpinia galanga*) and stinging nettle (*Urtica dioica*) provide reversal magic, while the black peppercorns (*Piper nigrum*) power the removal work.

MATERIALS

- ¾ cup (180 ml) sea salt (to neutralize)
- 3 tablespoons (45 ml) ground charcoal (for protection, to neutralize)
- 2 tablespoons (30 ml) black peppercorns (*Piper nigrum*) (for removal, reversal)
- 2 tablespoons (30 ml) galangal root (*Alpinia galanga*) (for justice work, reversal, to return to sender)
- 2 tablespoons (30 ml) stinging nettle (*Urtica dioica*) (for baneful magic, reversal, to return to sender)

Black Witches' Salt #3

This formula of black salt works best in baneful magic. That which has been sent to cause you harm is reversed and returned to the sender. The extra kick comes from you as justice for harm done.

MATERIALS

- ¾ cup (180 ml) sea salt (for absorption, neutralization)
- 2 tablespoons (30 ml) stinging nettle (*Urtica dioica*) (for baneful magic, protection, removal, reversal)
- 2 tablespoons (30 ml) ground black mustard seed (*Brassica nigra*) (for justice)
- ½ tablespoon (7 ml) devil's shoestring (*Viburnum alnifolium*) (for justice, protection)
- ½ tablespoon (7 ml) ground black peppercorns (*Piper nigrum*) (for protection, removal, reversal)

To Cause Someone's Life to Go to Garbage Curse

This spell is for when you really want to cause your target to endure a bad time and have everything go wrong.

Remember: When casting baneful magic, you need to be sure about your actions. Make sure you have no fault in the situation.

MATERIALS

- Stuffed doll
- Scissors

- Black Witches' Salt #3
- Sterile gloves
- 2 to 3 clumps of used cat litter
- Needle
- Thread

WORKING

1. Using the scissors, cut open the stuffed doll. Be sure to cut along at least half of a seam. You need to be able to easily reach inside of the doll.
2. Pull out the stuffing and bring it to the dirtiest section of the room. Stomp on the stuffing and grind it into the dirt. As you do so, focus all your feelings of anger, frustration, and so on toward your target into the dirt.
3. Put on the gloves and begin to fill the doll with the materials. Start with a small portion of the witches' salt.
4. Add a little of the stuffing back into the doll.
5. Break the used cat litter up into smaller chunks and add one of them to the doll.
6. Return some more of the stuffing to the doll.
7. Spit into the doll, stating:

   I curse (your target's name).

8. Repeat steps 3 through 7 until the doll is completely stuffed.

9. Use the needle and thread to stitch the doll closed. While you stitch the doll back together, chant:

    May your life turn upside down and go astray. There your life shall stay. When your lesson is learned, this curse shall go away, harming none from that day.

10. Toss the stuffed doll into a trash can away from your home. Know that as the doll travels to the dump, the curse is sent to your target and will remain until they learn not to cause harm to other people.

Green Witches' Salt

Green is a color of fertility and life. Adding a little bit of green salt to money spells boosts the power of the working. The green color in the following salts comes from shredded fake cash or herbs such as alfalfa.

GREEN WITCHES' SALT #1

One of the reasons this salt is so effective is the realistic toy money used to create the green color. This curio helps attract real money and wealth to your life.

MATERIALS

- ¾ cup (180 ml) sea salt (to neutralize blocks to success)

- 3 shredded bills of realistic-looking toy money (for money)
- 2 tablespoons (30 ml) alfalfa (*Medicago sativa*) (for fast cash, money)
- 1½ tablespoons (22 ml) pine needles (*Pinus* spp.) (for fertility, money, prosperity, success)
- ½ tablespoon (7 ml) dandelion leaves (*Taraxacum officinale*) (for money, wealth, wishes, success)

Attract Sales Working

This spell uses Green Witches' Salt #1 to attract new customers to your business and ensure that your regular customers keep returning.

I have sprinkled this powder around my tables and stalls at festivals and events to great effect, gaining new customers and seeing my regulars return.

MATERIALS

- Small magnet
- Green Witches' Salt #1

WORKING

1. Place the magnet in the register or near wherever sales and service fees are processed.
2. Sprinkle the witches' salt around the magnet. As you create a circle of salt around the magnet, state:

   Attract customers who are new, who will become regulars steady and true.

3. Take the remaining green salt and go outside your business. Sprinkle a path from the parking lot to your door. As you scatter the salt, repeat the statement from step 2. Repeat the statement until the path is completed.
4. As customers walk over this path, they will draw money and sales into your business.

Green Witches' Salt #2

This salt is an alternative to the first green salt, which uses shredded cash. This mixture uses herbal materials to get its green color instead. This version also focuses on bringing cash to you quickly.

MATERIALS

- ¾ cup (180 ml) sea salt (to remove blocks to success)
- 2½ tablespoons (37 ml) alfalfa (*Medicago sativa*) (for money, prosperity, success)
- 1 tablespoon (15 ml) basil (*Ocimum basilicum*) (for money, success)
- 1 tablespoon (15 ml) five-finger grass (*Potentilla canadensis*) (for fast cash, grabbing cash, money, prosperity, success)
- ½ tablespoon (7 ml) pine needles (*Pinus* spp.) (for money)

Green Witches' Salt #3

This third version of green witches' salt uses herbal, animal, and other curios to work effectively. Use this salt to empower any money spells or workings you do.

MATERIALS

- ¾ cup (180 ml) sea salt (to remove blocks to money)
- 2½ tablespoons (37 ml) five-finger grass (*Potentilla canadensis*) (for fast cash, money, prosperity)
- 3 shredded bills of realistic-looking toy money (for money, success)
- 1½ tablespoons (22 ml) basil (*Ocimum basilicum*) (for money, prosperity, success)
- 1 teaspoon (5 ml) bank dirt (for financial stability, money, success)
- 1 teaspoon (5 ml) dried ants or ant hill dirt (to remove blocks to financial stability, remove blocks to money)

Fast Cash Wallet Charm

This spell uses Witches' Green Salt #3 to ensure you have a steady flow of cash.

MATERIALS

- Dollar bill
- Small coin of your choice
- Green Witches' Salt #3
- 2 feet (.6 meters) green ribbon or thread

WORKING

1. Lay the dollar bill flat on your work surface. Place the coin in the center of the dollar bill.
2. Cover the coin with the witches' salt. As you cover the coin, state:

   Cash flowing toward me flows quite quickly.

3. Fold the bill around the coin so that the coin is covered by the bill, creating a packet.
4. Wrap the green ribbon or thread around the packet five times.
5. After the fifth wrap, tie a knot to secure the packet closed.
6. Keep the charm in your wallet to attract a steady flow of fast cash. To keep the charm active, sprinkle a layer of green salt over it once a week.
7. When you are ready to end the spell, cut the ribbon or thread and spend the cash. Dispose of the ribbon or thread in the trash.

Yellow Witches' Salt

Yellow salt relates to growth and prosperity. The color yellow is often symbolic of life and joy. As a symbol of life and joy, yellow is also often used to attract money, finances, and success.

Yellow Witches' Salt #1

This first version of yellow witchs' salt is designed to ensure that your success and prosperity will continue to grow.

Materials

- ¾ cup (180 ml) sea salt (to neutralize baneful energy directed at you)
- 2 tablespoons (30ml) sunflower petals (*Helianthus annuus*) (for growth, life, luck, money, success)
- 1½ tablespoons (22ml) goldenrod flowers (*Solidago altissima*) (for money, prosperity, success)
- ½ tablespoon (7 ml) Mexican marigold flowers (*Tagetes lemmonii*) (for money, prosperity, success)

Abundance & Prosperity Bowl Charm

This bowl charm uses Yellow Witches' Salt #1 to attract prosperity and abundance to your home. For best results, this bowl should be kept out in the open but remain undisturbed.

Materials

- Small bowl
- Pen
- Paper
- Yellow Witches' Salt #1
- 2 pieces of iron pyrite (for money, prosperity, wealth)

- 3 pieces of aventurine (for fertility, money, prosperity)
- 8-ounce (227-gram) package of shelled sunflower seeds (*Helianthus annuus*)

WORKING

1. On the paper, write out a petition for your home to have abundance, prosperity, and wealth.
2. Place your petition in the bottom of the bowl.
3. Cover the bottom of the bowl with the witches' salt.
4. Arrange the iron pyrite and aventurine in the bowl. Choose a placement that is pleasing to your eyes.
5. Once a day, add one sunflower seed to the bowl. As you add the sunflower seed, state:

   Abundance and prosperity come to me,
   wealth and prosperity growing freely.

6. Repeat step 5 until you run out of sunflower seeds. Once you run out of seeds, take the seeds from the bowl, remove them from their shells, and scatter them outside where birds and animals can eat them. This spreads the prosperity or wealth earned through the bowl into the greater world. (If needed, rinse the seeds to remove any lingering salt.)
7. To continue the bowl, remove the iron pyrite and aventurine and add a new layer of salt. Return the stones to their original positions. Dismantling

the bowl and disposing of the paper and salt in the trash ends the spell.

Yellow Witches' Salt #2

This salt uses the power of faith to bring you growth and success. By having faith in yourself and your projects, you are much more likely to have positive results.

MATERIALS

- 1 cup (250 ml) sea salt (to neutralize baneful energy directed at you)
- 2½ tablespoons (37 ml) yellow mustard seed (*Brassica alba*) (for faith, luck, prosperity, success)
- 1 tablespoon (15 ml) chamomile (*Matricaria recutita*) (for money, mood lifting, success)
- 1 tablespoon (15 ml) lemon balm (*Melissa officinalis*) (for prosperity, success, to remove blocks to success)
- ½ tablespoon (7 ml) bee pollen (for prosperity, success)

Yellow Witches' Salt #3

This powder works to ensure your business's success by bringing new customers to you. These customers will be loyal and will highly recommend the business.

MATERIALS

- 1 cup (250 ml) sea salt (to neutralize baneful energy directed at you)
- 2½ tablespoons (37 ml) goldenrod (*Solidago altissima*) (for money)
- 1½ tablespoons (22 ml) yarrow (*Achillea millefolium*) (to attract customers)
- ½ tablespoon (7 ml) sesame seeds (*Sesamum indicum*) (for money, prosperity, success, wealth)

Attract Customers Bottle Charm

Use this spell to attract customers to your business or place of work. The more customers you have, the more successful and prosperous your business will be.

MATERIALS

- Pen
- Paper
- Empty orange medication bottle
- Yellow Witches' Salt #3
- Iron pyrite tumble (for money, prosperity, success)
- Aventurine tumble (for money, prosperity, success)
- Alfalfa (*Medicago sativa*) (for fast cash)

WORKING

1. On the paper, write out a petition to attract customers and increase your sales.
2. Read the statement of intent, then carefully fold the petition and place it in the container.

3. Cover the petition with half of the yellow witches' salt.
4. Add the iron pyrite tumble to the bottle.
5. Add the aventurine tumble to the container.
6. Sprinkle the alfalfa over the tumbles.
7. Add the remaining yellow witches' salt to the bottle.
8. Seal the bottle with the cover, then begin to shake it. As you shake the bottle, repeat the following chant five to seven times:

    Customers that are new turn into customers true.

9. Hide the charm bottle by either the main entrance to your business or a cash register/point of sales system.
10. Once a day, repeat step 8 to keep the charm activated and charged.
11. When you are ready to end the spell, open the bottle and dispose of the herbal materials in the trash. The bottle, iron pyrite, and aventurine can be cleansed and used in future magical works.

Orange Salt

Orange salt is a great powder to use to boost your magic's success. Orange witches' salt contains all the magical properties of yellow witches' salt as well as passion, love, lust, and desire, which are properties of red witches' salt. Orange witches' salt can be used as a substitute for red or yellow salt depending on the type of spell you are doing and the results you desire.

Orange Witches' Salt #1

This orange salt attracts prosperity and love to your life and removes any blocks in the way to your success.

MATERIALS

- 1 cup (250 ml) sea salt (to remove blocks to success)
- 2½ tablespoons (37 ml) cinnamon (*Cinnamomum verum*) (for money, prosperity, to attract success, cleanse blocks)
- 2 tablespoons (30 ml) grains of paradise (*Aframomum melegueta*) (for good luck, prosperity, success)
- ½ tablespoon (7 ml) orange marigold flowers (*Calendula officinalis*) (for money, protection of success and money, success)

Orange Witches' Salt #2

Sometimes when things are going well in your life, you may find that people are jealous of your accomplishments. This blend of orange witches' salt allows your success to continue while entangling any baneful energy that has been directed at you and your achievements.

MATERIALS

- 1¼ cup (300 ml) sea salt (to neutralize baneful energy sent your way, removes blocks to success)
- 2 tablespoons (30 ml) ginger (*Zingiber officinale*) (for power, prosperity, success)
- 1½ tablespoons (22 ml) devil's shoestring (*Viburnum alnifolium*) (for protection from evil, to entangle baneful energy)
- ½ tablespoon (7 ml) allspice (*Pimenta dioica*) (for luck, prosperity, success)

Financial Growth Packet Spell

This small packet is about growing your finances. From gaining income to having fewer bills, the goal of this spell is to have more money coming in for immediate use and for savings.

MATERIALS

- Small envelope
- Pen
- Green colored pencil, marker, or pen
- 1 tablespoon (15 ml) bee pollen (for financial growth, money, success)
- 1 teaspoon (5 ml) sunflower (*Helianthus annuus*) (for growth, money, success, sun)
- Orange Witches' Salt #2

WORKING

1. On one side of the envelope, write the words "Financial Growth and Success." On the other side, write the words "Financial Security."

2. Sprinkle the bee pollen in the envelope. As you sprinkle the bee pollen, state:

    Bee pollen, my finances grow today. Growth and stability here to stay.

3. Add the sunflower seeds to the envelope. As you add the seeds, state:

    Like the sunflower grows to reach the sun, my journey for financial growth has just begun.

4. Add the witches' salt to the packet. As you add the salt, state:

    To ensure my success and prosperity continues and is protected from ill will.

5. Seal the envelope, then shake it vigorously to mix the materials. Once you have thoroughly shaken the envelope, keep it somewhere in your kitchen where it will be safe.

Orange Witches' Salt #3

This orange salt works like a combination of the previous two blends. It has the powder to attract luck, love, lust, and success.

Materials

- ¾ cup (180 ml) sea salt (to neutralize baneful energy, remove blocks)
- 1½ tablespoons (22 ml) orange zest (*Citrus sinensis*) (for love, luck, prosperity, success, to cleanse blocks)

- 1 tablespoon (15 ml) galangal root (*Alpinia galanga*) (for prosperity, success, to reflect and return baneful energy to sender)
- 1 tablespoon (15 ml) patchouli leaves (*Pogostemon cablin*) (for desire, lust, passion, sexuality)
- ½ tablespoon (7ml) devil's shoestring (*Viburnum alnifolium*) (for good luck, protection from evil, to entangle evil)

Open the Road to Sweet Luck Spell

This is a spell to bring you good luck. After working the spell, you may find yourself with friends, money, and opportunities that didn't exist before.

MATERIALS

- Pin, needle, or knife
- White taper candle
- Taper candleholder
- Orange Witches' Salt #3
- Thread or twine
- Skeleton key (for opportunities, to open roads, unlock doors)
- Personal effect
- Lighter or matches

WORKING

1. Use the pin, needle, or knife to carve the words "Good Luck" into two sides of the taper candle.
2. Rub the salt into the words you carved.

3. Set the candle into the candleholder.
4. Tie one end of the thread or twine around the middle of the taper candle. Tie the other end around the skeleton key and personal effect, letting the key and personal effect dangle from the candle. As you tie the personal effect and key together, state:

   I call upon the skeleton key. Unlock the doors so forward motion there may be.

5. Sprinkle the remaining salt in a circle around the base of the candleholder.
6. Light the candle, stating:

   By this candle's light, open doors are within my sight.

7. Let the candle burn for fifteen to thirty minutes. After that time, extinguish the candle.
8. Once a day, until the candle has completely burned, repeat steps 6 and 7.
9. When the candle burns the thread, place the key at the base of the candleholder and state:

   Roads that have been blocked, be now unlocked.

10. Once the candle has finished burning and the wax is cool to the touch, dispose of the candle remains, personal effect, and salt at the base of the candleholder. Carry the skeleton key with you as a good luck charm.

Red Salt

Red salt is perfect for any love and relationship work. Depending on which herbs you choose to include in a red salt, you can make one that is more focused on lust and desire or one that is focused more on romance.

Red Witches' Salt #1

This form of red salt is sweet and spicy, which is just what a deep, long-term romantic relationship should be. The sweetness is for love and attraction, and the spice is for lust and desire.

MATERIALS

- 1 cup (250 ml) sea salt (to absorb love energy and help distribute the power in the finished salt)
- 2½ tablespoons (37 ml) red rose petals (*Rosa rubiginosa*) (for love, lust, relationships, romance)
- 1 tablespoon (15 ml) cayenne pepper (*Capsicum annuum*) (for passion, sexuality)
- 1 tablespoon (15 ml) cinnamon (*Cinnamomum verum*) (for desire, love, passion, romance, sweetness)
- ½ tablespoon (7 ml) paprika (for desire, love, romance, sweetness)

Love for Me Petition & Candle Spell

This spell combines the power of burning a petition with that of Red Witches' Salt #1 to attract love into your life.

MATERIALS

- Fire extinguisher or bowl of water
- 3 pieces of paper
- Pin, needle, or knife
- Red taper candle
- Lighter or matches
- Firesafe bowl or cauldron
- Taper candleholder
- ½ cup (125 ml) Red Witches' Salt #1
- Spoon or wand
- Broom
- Dustpan

WORKING

1. For fire safety, set the bowl of water or fire extinguisher near your workspace.
2. On one of the pieces of paper, write out a petition that describes the kind of relationship you want and the type of person you want to have the relationship with. Rewrite the petition until you feel it is perfect.
3. On the second and third pieces of paper, write out two clean versions of the perfected petition. Take one of the final drafts and cross out every duplicated letter in the petition. Make a list of the remaining letters. If no letters remain from the original petition, reword the petition to have remaining letters.
4. Create a sigil by arranging the remaining letters into a design that you find appealing. Try as many

designs as you can come up with until you find the one you like the most. Circle or make a note of the final sigil design you have selected.

5. Draw the chosen sigil under the clean petition, then use the pin, needle, or knife to carve the sigil into the candle.
6. Read the petition aloud and place the petition with the sigil in the bowl.
7. Light the candle. Use the flame of the candle to light the petition on fire.
8. Place the candle in the holder. Let the candle and paper burn.
9. Once the ashes have cooled, add the witches' salt to the bowl. Use the spoon or wand to stir and combine the ashes and salt. As you stir the materials, repeat the following chant seven to nine times:

    Love new, love true.

10. Once everything is combined thoroughly, use the broom and dustpan to distribute the powder from your driveway or sidewalk up to your front door. Every step taken across this mixture will attract love into your life.

Red Witches' Salt #2

Use this salt in spells to manifest lust in your life.

MATERIALS

- 1 cup (250 ml) sea salt (to absorb love energy and help distribute the power in the finished salt)
- 2½ tablespoons (37 ml) cayenne pepper (*Capsicum annuum*) (for desire, fire, lust, passion)
- 1 tablespoon (15 ml) clove (*Syzygium aromaticum*) (for desire, lust)
- 1 tablespoon (15 ml) grains of paradise (*Aframomum melegueta*) (for attraction, desire, love, lust, passion)
- ½ tablespoon (7 ml) powdered dragon's blood (*Dracaena cinnabari*) (for desire, lust, passion, sexuality)

Satisfy My Lust Candle Spell

Use this spell to ensure that when you lust after someone or something, your desire can be met and taken care of.

MATERIALS

- Red or orange chime candle
- Pin, needle, or knife
- Chime candleholder
- Red Witches' Salt #2
- Lighter or matches

WORKING

1. Take the chime candle in one hand. With the other, use the pin, needle, or knife to carve the word "Desire" into the candle.
2. Rub some of the red salt on the candle where you carved the word.
3. Set the candle in the holder.
4. Sprinkle the remaining salt around the candleholder. As you sprinkle the salt, state:

   Powder of lust, to manifest my desire is a must.

5. Light the candle. As you do so, state:

   Candle that is burning bright, set my desires alight.

6. Let the candle burn completely.
7. When the candle has burned down, toss the candle's remains and the salt into the trash and walk away. The rest is in the hands of the universe.

RED WITCHES' SALT #3

This red salt focuses on friendship over romance. Many romantic partnerships often start with a deep friendship, and a strong partnership should have friendship as a deep component of the relationship.

MATERIALS

- 1 cup (250 ml) sea salt (to absorb love energy and help distribute the power in the finished salt)

- 2 tablespoons (30 ml) red rose petals (*Rosa rubiginosa*) (for all forms of love)
- 1½ tablespoons (22 ml) catnip (*Nepeta cataria*) (for friendship, happiness, love)
- 1 tablespoon (15 ml) passionflower (*Passiflora incarnata*) (for friendship, love, romance)
- ½ tablespoon (7 ml) allspice (*Pimenta dioica*) (for friendship, love, relationships)

Blue Witches' Salt

Blue witches' salt is a tool often used in healing spells and communication work. It works well as a poppet or bottle filling. Blue salt is one of the only witches' salts to use food coloring to achieve its color. Blue coloring can also be created by using crushed blue seashells or by adding baking powder to some boiled red cabbage broth. The mixture of baking powder and red cabbage broth dries into a blue powder that can be used to color your salts.

Natural Blue Dye

Follow these instructions to make your own natural blue dye. This dry dye can be used just like food coloring to bring blue color to your powders.

MATERIALS:

- About ½ of a head of red cabbage, chopped
- Pot
- Water
- Strainer

- Bowl
- Mixing spoon
- About ¼ teaspoon (1 ml) baking powder (Baking soda can be used instead if needed.)
- Storage container

WORKING

1. Place the chopped cabbage into the pot.
2. Fill the pot with enough water to cover the cabbage leaves.
3. Set the pot on the stove and bring the water to a boil.
4. Once boiling, reduce the heat to a simmer for about 15 minutes. You want the water to have a deep purple color.
5. Strain the water into the bowl and compost the cabbage solids.
6. Return the water to the pot and set it to simmer on low heat to reduce the mixture. You want the liquid to reduce by roughly ⅓ to ½ the original volume.
7. Remove the pot from the heat and let the liquid cool completely.
8. Once the liquid has cooled completely, slowly stir in the baking powder a little bit at a time, until the powder has reached a satisfactory shade of blue.
9. Store the finished dye.

Blue Witches' Salt #1

When it comes to healing, it is easy to overlook the connections between the mind, body, and spirit. This blue witches' salt helps heal all aspects of the self at once, providing true holistic healing.

MATERIALS

- 1½ cup (375 ml) sea salt (for cleansing, neutralization of any baneful energy, removal)
- Blue food coloring
- 2 tablespoons (30 ml) lavender (*Lavandula officinalis*) (for blue color, healing)
- 1½ tablespoons (37 ml) allheal (*Prunella vulgaris*) (for healing)
- 1 tablespoon (15 ml) lemon balm (*Melissa officinalis*) (for cleansing, healing, removal of blocks to health, spiritual cleansing)
- 1 tablespoon (15 ml) rosemary (*Salvia rosmarinus*) (for communication, healing)
- ½ tablespoon (7 ml) peppermint (*Mentha piperita*) (for healing)

Healing Candle Spell

Use this candle spell to heal your mind, body, and spirit.

MATERIALS

- Photo of the individual who needs healing
- Pen
- Small plate

- Blue Witches' Salt #1
- Taper candleholder
- Blue taper candle
- Pin, needle, or knife
- Lighter or matches

WORKING

1. On the back of the photo, write the name and date of birth of the individual who needs healing. If no photo is available, simply write their name, their date of birth, and what needs healing on a piece of paper.
2. Place the photo face up on the small plate and cover it with the salt.
3. Set the candleholder on top of the salt.
4. Use the pin, needle, or knife to carve the word "Heal" into two sides of the candle, then place the candle in the holder.
5. Light the candle. As you do so, state:

   By this candle's light, great health and wellness is insight.

6. Let the candle burn for ten to fifteen minutes, then extinguish the candle flame.
7. Once a day, until the candle has fully burned, light the candle and repeat the statement from step 5, letting it burn for another ten to fifteen minutes.
8. When the candle has completely burned, dispose of the candle remains, salt, and photo in the trash.

Blue Witches' Salt #2

This blue witches' salt is designed to help a person slow down and rest so they can heal.

MATERIALS

- ¾ cup (180 ml) sea salt (for cleansing, removal of healing blocks)
- Blue food coloring
- 2 tablespoons (30 ml) lavender (*Lavandula officinalis*) (for blue color, healing, peace, rest, sleep)
- 1 tablespoon (15 ml) chamomile (*Matricaria recutita*) (for healing, rest, sleep)
- 1 tablespoon (15 ml) peppermint (*Mentha piperita*) (for healing, relaxation)

Blue Witches' Salt #3

This blue salt excels when used in spells that deal with mental health. The herbs focus on healing, focus, mental clarity, and raising energetic vibrations to help boost mood. This helps make symptoms easier to manage.

MATERIALS

- 1 cup (250 ml) sea salt (for cleansing, healing, removal of blocks)
- Blue food coloring
- 2½ tablespoons (37 ml) lavender (*Lavandula officinalis*) (for anxiety relief, blue color, depression relief, healing)

- 1 tablespoon (15 ml) lemon balm (*Melissa officinalis*) (for anxiety relief, depression relief, focus, healing, restlessness relief)
- 1 tablespoon (15 ml) Saint-John's-wort (*Hypericum perforatum*) (for depression relief, healing, mood stabilization)
- ½ tablespoon (7 ml) ginkgo leaves (*Ginkgo biloba*) (for clarity of thought, healing, mental focus)

SELF-HEALING POPPET SPELL

This poppet spell uses blue salt #3 and your personal effects to promote healing for yourself. Use this spell for mental health healing, as well as for physical healing.

Note that the amount of materials listed here is a guideline. You may need more or less depending on the size of your poppet.

MATERIALS

- Two pieces of 6 × 6-inch (15 × 15-cm) white fabric (Cotton is best, but any material works.)
- Pen
- Scissors
- Needle
- 2 feet (61 cm) blue thread
- Personal effect (Hair or fingernail clippings work best, but a scrap of old clothing can also work.)
- 2 tablespoons (30 ml) lavender (*Lavandula officinalis*) (for healing)

- 2 tablespoons (30 ml) peppermint (*Mentha piperita*) (for healing)
- Blue Witches' Salt #3
- Poly-fil stuffing, optional (Use stuffing if you want a fluffy or full poppet.)

WORKING

1. Place the two pieces of fabric on top of each other. Draw a rough human shape on the top piece.
2. Cut along the shape you just drew, cutting through both layers of fabric. This makes the two halves of your poppet.
3. Thread the needle and begin to stitch the poppet together. Use a simple in-and-out, back-to-front stitch. The stitches do not have to look perfect. They just have to be effective, keeping the material together.
4. While stitching the poppet together, recite Psalm 103:1–5 until you have sewn all but a small opening at the head of the poppet:

   Praise the Lord, my soul;
   all my inmost being, praise his holy name.
   Praise the Lord, my soul,
   and forget not all his benefits—
   who forgives all your sins
   and heals all your diseases,
   who redeems your life from the pit
   and crowns you with love and compassion,
   who satisfies your desires with good things

> ***so that your youth is renewed like the eagle's.***[4]

5. Add the personal effect to the poppet. As you place your effect in the poppet, state:

    Poppet, I name you after me today. With me, all healing shall stay.

6. Add the remaining materials to the poppet one at a time, asking each material for its assistance with your healing work. If you are using stuffing to create a more plush poppet, add it now, alternating the stuffing with the other materials.
7. Finish stitching the poppet closed.
8. Inhale deeply. Exhale over the poppet. State:

    With this breath, I give you life. The energy found within thee shall thus be sent over to me.

9. Set the completed poppet somewhere you will see it every day and it will not be disturbed.
10. For ten to fifteen minutes every day, cuddle, hold, and play with the poppet. The more time and energy you spend playing with the poppet, the more healing energy will be sent your way.
11. When you have received all the healing that you need, use the scissors to cut the poppet up. The cutting of the threads ends the spell. Dispose of the poppet pieces in the trash.

---

4. Psalm 103:1–5.

Purple Witches' Salt

Purple witches' salt is great for any psychic or deep spiritual work. Whether you wish to reach a light meditative state or access deeper trance states and perform underworld work, purple witches' salt is a great aid in all psychic or spiritual work that involves an altered state of consciousness. The purple color either comes from flowers such as African violets and lavender or food coloring.

Purple Witches' Salt #1

This witches' salt is all about psychic sight and mental powers. Meditation, divination, deep trance work, scrying—this witches' salt can be used for all of the above. The purple in this salt comes from lavender flowers.

MATERIALS

- ¾ cup (180 ml) sea salt (for cleansing, removing blocks to psychic sight)
- 2 tablespoons (30 ml) lavender (*Lavandula officinalis*) (for mental clarity, mental focus, psychic powers)
- 1 tablespoon (15 ml) mugwort (*Artemisia vulgaris*) (for divination, psychic development, psychic powers, trance work)
- ½ tablespoon (7 ml) eyebright (*Euphrasia rostkoviana*) (for psychic sight, spiritual sight, mental powers)
- ½ tablespoon (7 ml) lemongrass (*Cymbopogon citratus*) (for psychic powers)

Crystal Ball Cleanse & Empower Spell

Crystal balls have long been associated with psychic power and psychic work. This spell uses Purple Witches' Salt #1 to cleanse and empower your crystal ball for scrying work.

MATERIALS

- Clear bowl of water
- Crystal ball
- Crystal ball stand
- Small plate
- Purple silk, satin, or cotton covering cloth
- Purple Witches' Salt #1

WORKING

1. Using the bowl of water, wash the crystal ball. As you wash the crystal ball, state:

    Cleanse and bless this crystal ball. Open my psychic sight to details great and small.

2. Place the crystal ball on its stand. Set the stand on the small plate.
3. Sprinkle the witches' salt around the crystal ball's stand. As you sprinkle the salt, state:

    Purple witches' salt, on this night, empower my crystal for true psychic sight.

4. Cover the crystal ball with the covering cloth and set the plate aside where it will not be disturbed. Leave the ball there for forty-eight hours.

5. After forty-eight hours, whenever you are ready to use this crystal ball, sprinkle a bit more of the purple salt around the crystal ball's stand. This will activate the power within the crystal. Repeat as needed when working with your crystal ball.

Purple Witches' Salt #2

Use this salt to help open your psychic senses for more clarity and understanding. The purple coloring in this salt comes from African violets. This simple flower has a small but potent life force.

MATERIALS

- 1¼ cup (310 ml) sea salt (to cleanse blocks to psychic sight)
- 2 tablespoons (30 ml) African violet flowers (*Saintpaulia ionantha*) (for mental focus, psychic power, psychic, senses, psychic sight)
- 2 tablespoons (30 ml) lavender (*Lavandula officinalis*) (for concentration, mental focus, peace of mind)
- 1 tablespoon (15 ml) eyebright (*Euphrasia rostkoviana*) (for mental powers, psychic sight, spiritual sight)
- ½ tablespoon (7 ml) ginkgo leaves (*Ginkgo biloba*) (for mental clarity, mental focus)
- ½ tablespoon (7 ml) rosemary (*Salvia rosmarinus*) (for memory, mental powers, psychic senses)

Purple Witches' Salt #3

This salt will help keep you protected from spiritual attacks and getting lost while doing underworld work or engaging in astral travel. This powder also helps provide clear sight and will help you remember what happened during your astral or underworld travels.

MATERIALS

- 1¼ cup (310 ml) sea salt (to cleanse blocks to psychic sight, protect against spirits)
- 2 tablespoons (30 ml) African violet flowers (*Saintpaulia ionantha*) (for mental focus, psychic senses, psychic power)
- 2 tablespoons (30 ml) lavender (*Lavandula officinalis*) (for mental focus, peace, protection, psychic abilities)
- 1 tablespoon (15 ml) rosemary (*Salvia rosmarinus*) (for memory, mental focus, mental powers, psychic abilities)
- ½ tablespoon (7 ml) arnica flowers (*Arnica montana*) (for protection from spiritual forces, to increase psychic powers)
- ½ tablespoon (7 ml) wormwood (*Artemisia absinthium*) (for astral travel, psychic work, spiritual development)

Underworld Travels Charm

Traveling through the underworld and connecting to the spirits of the dead is one of the many ways we can communicate with our ancestors and other spirits. This charm is a tool that provides you easier access to trance states and the underworld. The Ancestor Blessings Powder can be found in chapter 5, "Common Magical Powders."

MATERIALS

- Skeleton key (to open the doors to the underworld)
- Small bottle large enough to fit the skeleton key (Used pill bottles are perfect for this spell.)
- Purple Witches' Salt #3
- Ancestor Blessings Powder
- 2 feet (61 cm) necklace chain
- Pen
- Sticker label

WORKING

1. Place the skeleton key in the bottle. As you place the key in the bottle, state:

   Skeleton key, open the underworld door for me.

2. Add the witches' salt to the bottle. State:

   Purple witches' salt, protect me as through the underworld I travel freely.

3. Add the Ancestor Blessings Powder to the bottle. State:

   Ancestors, on this day, through the underworld show me the way.

4. Seal the bottle.

5. Shake the bottle vigorously. While you shake the bottle, repeat the following statement seven to nine times:

   Traveling in the underworld I go, my wisdom and knowledge through this journey does grow.

6. Open the bottle and remove the key from the bottle. Place the key on the chain. Reseal the bottle and label it "Underworld Travels Charm Powder."

7. Whenever you do trance work that deals with the underworld, wear or hold the skeleton key for easy access and guidance during those sessions.

8. Once a month, return the key to the bottle, seal the bottle, and shake the bottle while repeating the same statement used in step 5.

Gray Salt

Gray witches' salt protects and neutralizes any unwanted energy sent your way. Using gray salt in this manner is the same as applying plain sea salt or a witches' black salt. Gray salt combines the charcoal or ash of black salt with a material such as cascarilla powder for cleansing and protection.

Alternatively gray salt can be used in baneful workings, such as mirror and return-to-sender magic. It is no different than using mace or a taser in self-defense. Sometimes a little force is needed to protect yourself.

Gray Witches' Salt #1

This salt neutralizes any evil or ill will sent your way. When using this salt, only energy that you want or find useful will be allowed into your home.

MATERIALS

- ¾ cup (180 ml) sea salt (for cleansing, to neutralize baneful energy)
- 5 tablespoons (75 ml) cascarilla powder (for protection)
- 1 tablespoon (15 ml) anvil dust (for protection)
- 1 tablespoon (15 ml) ash (to neutralize baneful energy)
- 1 tablespoon (15 ml) black peppercorns (*Piper nigrum*) (for removal, reversal)

Gray Witches' Salt #2

Use this version of gray salt to reflect and neutralize any unwanted energy.

MATERIALS

- ¾ cup (180 ml) sea salt (for cleansing, to neutralize baneful energy)
- 2 tablespoons (30 ml) black peppercorns (*Piper nigrum*) (for baneful magic, reflection, removal, reversal)
- 1 tablespoon (15 ml) stinging nettle leaves (*Urtica dioica*) (for cleansing, protection, removal, to return to sender)

- ½ tablespoon (7 ml) valerian root (*Valeriana officinalis*) (for banishing, protection, removal, to reflect evil)
- 5 cat's eye shells (for protection, to reflect back, repel evil)

Gray Witches' Salt #3

This gray salt is more of a baneful powder than a protective powder. When applying this salt, magical attacks that are sent your way are reflected back to the sender, protecting you and hurting those who would have otherwise harmed you at the same time.

MATERIALS

- 1½ cup (375 ml) sea salt (for cleansing, protection from baneful energy, to neutralize baneful energy sent your way)
- 3 tablespoons (45 ml) black peppercorns (*Piper nigrum*) (to reflect, return to sender)
- 2 tablespoons (30 ml) poppy seeds (*Papaver somniferum*) (for chaos, confusion)
- 1½ tablespoons (22 ml) black mustard seeds (*Brassica nigra*) (for chaos, confusion, protection)
- ½ tablespoons (7ml) stinging nettle leaves (*Urtica dioica*) (for protection, removal, to return to sender)

Pocket Reflect & Reverse Charm

This is a small charm that you can carry with you in your pocket, purse, or any bag you happen to have with you. Any baneful or unwanted magical work that is sent to you will be reflected to its sender.

MATERIALS

- Two-sided compact mirror
- Personal effects
- Gray Witches' Salt #3
- Ivy (*Hedera helix*) (to entangle evil)
- Thorns
- Hot glue gun or superglue

WORKING

1. Set one personal effect on one side of the compact mirror. As you place the personal effect, state:

    Effect of mine, one this day, take all attacks sent back and from me away.

2. Cover that first effect with the gray witchs' salt. As you add the salt, state:

    Witches' salt that is gray, neutralize and reflect baneful effects sent my way.

3. Place the ivy vine on top of the salt. As you do so, state:

    Vine, use your powers divine to entangle evil and bind it through in you being entwined.

4. Set the thorns on top of the vines. State:

   Thorns, tear, destroy, and attack that which cannot be sent back.

5. Line the edges of the compact with glue.
6. Close the compact and press the sides together. The glue should hold the sides together. Set the compact somewhere the glue can dry for forty-eight hours.
7. Once the glue is dry, carry the charm with you for protection against evil and magical attacks sent your way.
8. When you feel the charm has done its job and you no longer need its protection, take the charm outside and destroy it. Hitting the charm with a hammer is ideal, but any method of destruction works. Toss the remains in the trash to release the spell.

Sweetening Magical Powders

Many sweetening powders can be used to help bring peace into your life, keeping the house running smoothly and other issues at bay. From encouraging people to listen to you to attracting others to you, sweetening magic is a powerful tool.

Influencing Powders

One of the uses of sweetening powders is to influence the way individuals think about you and your point of view. Sometimes these powders are labeled as controlling powders, but it's not really control. The individuals targeted still have complete freedom over their choices and actions. Your thoughts and actions are simply more of an influence than they may have otherwise been.

Look at Me Love & Lust Powder

Love and lust powders are two of the most common types of influencing powders. I have included more love and lust powders later in the chapter in their own section. This one is here to demonstrate its use. Note that the only difference between a love powder and a lust powder is the intent behind it. The same herbs are often used.

MATERIALS

- 1 cup (250 ml) sugar (*Saccharum officinarum*) (for attraction, desire, love, lust, passion, sweetness)
- 2½ tablespoons (37 ml) damiana leaves (*Turnera diffusa*) (for love, lust)
- 1 tablespoon (15 ml) cardamom (*Elettaria cardamomum*) (for love, lust)
- 1 tablespoon (15 ml) lemongrass (*Cymbopogon citratus*) (for desire, lust)
- ½ tablespoon (7 ml) rosemary (*Salvia rosmarinus*) (for attraction, love, to open the mind)

Stop Behavior Powder

Sometimes people engage in behaviors that are dangerous, unhealthy, or otherwise problematic. Use this powder when you are trying to get someone to stop those behaviors.

MATERIALS

- ¾ cup (180 ml) sugar (*Saccharum officinarum*) (to get people to listen to you, open up the mind, sweeten)
- 2½ tablespoons (37 ml) masterwort (*Astrantia major*) (for control, power, protection from old behaviors)
- 1½ tablespoons (22 ml) rosemary (*Salvia rosmarinus*) (for healing, to open the mind)
- 1 teaspoon (5 ml) stop sign dirt (to stop actions)
- 6 snail shells (for protection, to slow down, stop)

Listen to Me Powder

This powder can be used when you need someone to listen to what you have to say. Use this in courtrooms, during home discussions, and at work. This powder helps ensure that your voice is heard and what you say is taken into consideration.

MATERIALS

- ¾ cup (180 ml) sugar (*Saccharum officinarum*) (to open the mind, sweeten)
- 2½ tablespoons (37 ml) masterwort (*Astrantia major*) (for confidence, control, power)
- 1½ tablespoons (22 ml) rosemary (*Salvia rosmarinus*) (for mental focus, to open the mind)
- ½ tablespoon (7 ml) plantain leaves (*Plantago major*) (for power, strength)
- 4 acorn tops (*Quercus* spp.) (for strength, power, protection)

Stop Problematic Behavior Candle Spell

The following work uses both Listen To Me Powder and Stop Behavior Powder to get someone you love to stop engaging in behaviors that are dangerous or troublesome. Only perform this spell after trying all other methods to get them to stop those behaviors.

MATERIALS

- Pen
- Index card
- 8 pins
- Small heat-safe dinner plate
- Pin, needle, or knife
- Black votive candle
- Listen to Me Powder
- Stop Behavior Powder
- Lighter or matches

WORKING

1. On the index card, draw out a large octagon or stop sign. Make sure the shape is large enough for the votive candle to sit comfortably within it. In the center of the octagon, write the words "Stop Behavior." Under "Stop Behavior," write out the name and date of birth of the individual whose behavior you are trying to stop and what behavior needs to stop.

2. Place the index card on the plate. Stab a needle into one of the corners of the octagon. As you stab the pin into the octagon, state:

   Stop (behavior) is what I ask. This behavior cannot last.

3. Repeat step 2 at each of the remaining octagon corners.

4. Use the pin, needle, or knife to carve the word "Stop" into two sides of the candle. Place the candle in center of the octagon.

5. Sprinkle a layer of the Listen To Me Powder around the candle. As you sprinkle the powder, state:

   (Name of individual), today listen to what I have to say. (Behavior) is bad for you, making you to yourself not true.

6. Sprinkle a layer of Stop Behavior Powder around the candle. As you sprinkle the powder, state:

   Stop your behavior and bad act. Stop (behavior) and I will welcome you back.

7. Light the candle. As you do so, state:

   By this candle's soft light, healing for (name of individual) is in sight.

8. Let the candle burn for fifteen minutes. After fifteen minutes, extinguish the candle.

9. The next day, before you relight the candle, sprinkle a little more of the Stop Behavior Powder

around the candle. As you sprinkle the powder, repeat the statement from step 6.

10. Repeat step 7 and let the candle burn for ten to fifteen minutes, then extinguish.
11. Repeat steps 9 and 10 once a day until the candle has fully burned.
12. Once the candle has burned completely and the wax is cool to the touch, remove the pins from the paper. Dispose of the paper, wax, and powder in a trash can. This ends the spell—and their bad behavior.

Employment Powders

Sweetening powders can also be used in employment spells. From attracting a business you want to work for to gaining a promotion or even landing a new job, sweetening powders can be used.

Interview Confidence Powder

This powder works to boost your confidence when going through the interview process, opening potential employers' eyes to your best qualities.

MATERIALS

- ¾ cup (180 ml) sugar (*Saccharum officinarum*) (for attraction, sweetness, success)

- 1½ tablespoons (22 ml) gravel root (*Eutrochium purpureum*) (for influence over employment, to gain employment)
- 1 tablespoon (15 ml) allspice (*Pimenta dioica*) (for luck, money, prosperity)
- 1 tablespoon (15 ml) chamomile (*Matricaria recutita*) (for money, protection of money, sweetness, to open the mind)
- ½ tablespoon (7 ml) rosemary (*Salvia rosmarinus*) (for confidence, to open the mind)

Employ Me, Please Pocket Charm

Cast this spell the night before you have a job interview to increase your confidence and boost your chances of landing the job.

MATERIALS

- 2 business cards from the business or individual you will interview for
- Pen
- Slip of paper
- Interview Confidence Powder
- Rosemary sprig (*Salvia rosmarinus*) (for confidence, to get people to listen to you, open the mind)
- 3–5 feet (1–1.5 meters) yellow ribbon
- 3–5 feet (1–1.5 meters) green ribbon

WORKING

1. Set the first business card face down so the back is facing you.

2. On the paper, write the statement: "Employed at/by (business you are interviewing for)."
3. Place the paper with your statement on top of the first business card.
4. Cover your statement of intent with the Interview Confidence Powder. As you cover the statement, state:

   All the questions I am asked, I answer confidently and fast.

5. Carefully place the sprig of rosemary on top of the powder. State:

   Open the mind that they may see the asset I will surely be.

6. Set the second business card face up on top of the pile.
7. Wrap the yellow ribbon widthwise around the business card pile, repeating the following chant until the ribbon runs out:

   I ace today, confident and true, to land a job that is new.

8. Wrap the green ribbon around the packet lengthwise, repeating the following chant:

   A new job for me brings money and prosperity.

9. When the green ribbon nears the end, tie it in a knot to seal the packet. The charm is now ready to be carried with you.

10. In the morning, before you go to the interview, dust the packet with a pinch of the Interview Confidence Powder.
11. Carry the packet in your pocket when you go to the interview. While you wait for the interview, play with the packet. The energy in the packet will be transferred to your hands and body.
12. When you land the job you are interviewing for, you can dispose of the charm. Use scissors to cut the ribbon and toss the packet in the trash. This will release the spell.

Attract a Future Employer Powder

This powder works best when you are trying to bring a business that you really want to work for to your area. This works for chain stores as well as larger businesses and corporate entities.

MATERIALS

- ¾ cup (180 ml) sugar (*Saccharum officinarum*) (for attraction)
- 2 tablespoons (30 ml) gravel root (*Eutrochium purpureum*) (for employment)
- 1 tablespoon (15 ml) grains of paradise (*Aframomum melegueta*) (for employment, luck, money, success)
- 1 tablespoon (15 ml) Mexican marigold flowers (*Tagetes lemmonii*) (for employment, money, to protect wealth)

- ½ teaspoon (2.5 ml) dirt from the business (business card ashes can substitute) (to represent the business)
- ½ teaspoon (2.5 ml) dirt from a crossroads (for attraction, to send energy in the four cardinal directions)

Promote Me Powder

This powder works best when you are trying to gain a promotion at work. Only use this powder if you hold the qualifications for the position in question.

MATERIALS

- 1 cup (250 ml) sugar (*Saccharum officinarum*) (for attraction, money, prosperity, sweetness)
- 2½ tablespoons (37 ml) masterwort (*Astrantia major*) (for control, influence of direct actions)
- 1½ tablespoons (22 ml) gravel root (*Eutrochium purpureum*) (for employment, money, prosperity)
- ½ tablespoon (7 ml) chamomile (*Matricaria recutita*) (for money, protection of money, sweetness, to open the mind)
- ½ tablespoon (7 ml) rosemary (*Salvia rosmarinus*) (for influence, money, success, to open the mind)

Promotion Candle Spell

This candle spell is designed to help you obtain promotions you are eligible for. When working this spell, make sure you meet all the qualifications required for the job.

MATERIALS

- Small firesafe bowl
- Fire extinguisher or bowl of water
- Chime candleholder
- Orange chime candle
- Promote Me Powder
- Dirt from your place of employment
- Lighter or matches
- Business card of your boss/employer (A piece of paper with their name and position works as a substitute.)
- Spoon or wand
- Small plastic baggie or used spice jar
- Pen
- Sticker label
- Small broom or fan

WORKING

1. Set the chime candleholder in front of the bowl and place the chime candle in the holder. For safety, place the fire extinguisher or bowl of water next to your work area.
2. Combine the Promote Me Powder and the dirt from your job in the bowl. As you combine the powder and dirt, state:

   A promotion for me, success there will be.

3. Light the candle. As you do so, state:

   As this candle does burn, a promotion do I earn.

4. Use the fire from the candle to set the business card on fire. Carefully drop the burning business card into the bowl.
5. After the ashes have cooled, use the spoon or wand to mix the ashes, dirt, and powder together.
6. Once the materials are thoroughly combined, use the spoon or wand to move the powder from the bowl to the baggie or spice jar. Label it.
7. The next time you go to work, bring the container of powder with you. Use the small broom or fan to dust the powder around your boss's office as well as the rest of the business. As your boss and other individuals walk through the powder, the energy will be spread and activated, getting them to consider you for the promotion.

Fast Cash Powders

Use these fast cash powders in workings to sweeten your relationship with money. These powders make it easier for money to come your way. They encourage people to help you or give you money.

Dirty Fast Cash Powder

Use this powder when you need to attract money fast. This formula uses the power of place and the sweetness of sugar to bring you cash quickly.

MATERIALS

- ¾ cup (180 ml) sugar (*Saccharum officinarum*) (for attraction, money, prosperity, speed, sweetness)
- 1 tablespoon (15 ml) alfalfa (*Medicago sativa*) (for fast cash)
- 1 tablespoon (15 ml) cinquefoil (*Potentilla canadensis*) (for fast cash)
- 1 tablespoon (15 ml) pine needles (*Pinus* spp.) (for fertility, money, prosperity)
- 2 teaspoons (10 ml) dirt from a bank (for financial security, money)

Fast-Flowing Money Powder

When working with this magical powder, you will have a fast-flowing, steady supply of money. This can be through work, winning contests, or even just gifts.

MATERIALS

- 1 cup (250 ml) sugar (*Saccharum officinarum*) (for attraction, money, sweetness)
- 1 tablespoon (15 ml) chamomile (*Matricaria recutita*) (for luck, money, prosperity, success)
- 1 tablespoon (15 ml) fenugreek (*Trigonella foenum-graecum*) (for attraction, money, prosperity)

- 1 tablespoon (15 ml) pine needles (*Pinus* spp.) (for constant money flow, money, prosperity, success through hardships)
- 1 tablespoon (15 ml) yellow mustard seed (*Brassica alba*) (for luck, money, prosperity)

Sweet Fast Cash Powder

Having money that comes to you quickly is sweet. This powder uses the power of sweet and spicy flavors to bring you cash fast.

Materials

- 1 cup (250 ml) sugar (*Saccharum officinarum*) (for attraction, money, prosperity, sweetness)
- 2½ tablespoons (37 ml) cinnamon (*Cinnamomum verum*) (for fast cash, money, prosperity, speed, sweetness)
- 1½ tablespoons (22 ml) nutmeg (*Myristica fragrans*) (for luck, money, prosperity)
- 1 tablespoon (15 ml) allspice (*Pimenta dioica*) (for fast cash)
- 1 tablespoon (15 ml) galangal root (*Alpinia galanga*) (for fertility, money, prosperity)

Fast Cash Coin Tower Charm

Create this charm when your spirits are down and times are tough. This charm will attract what you need to get through the situation and thrive.

MATERIALS

- Coins in 5 different sizes (Flat stones can be used as a substitute, but coins work better.)
- Sweet Fast Cash Powder
- Honey or pine sap (*Pinus* spp.) (for money, prosperity, success, to stick money to you)

WORKING

1. Lay the coins face up in your work area.
2. Sprinkle the powder over the coins. As you sprinkle the powder, state:

   Money flowing fast and free, come this way and stick to me.

3. In the center of all but the smallest coin, place a dab of the honey or sap and state:

   Pine sap, which works like glue, brings financial security new and true.

4. Stack the coins on top of each other, placing the largest coin on the bottom and the smallest on top.
5. Repeat step 2 over the coin tower.
6. Place the coin tower somewhere in your home where it will not be disturbed. As long as the coin tower remains, you will be able to obtain all the cash you need quickly.

Healing Powders

Healing magic is one of my favorite types of magical work to do. My first highly effective spells and rituals were those that dealt with healing. The following powders attract healing and bring a sense of peace and calm, as you will know your health is being taken care of.

Sweet Healing Powder

While sugar and sweetness are not necessarily things that many people would associate with healing and good health, sugar does many things for the body. The mental health boost provided by this powder allows the body to relax and heal as needed.

MATERIALS

- ¾ cup (180 ml) allheal (*Prunella vulgaris*) (for healing, health, wellness)
- 1½ tablespoons (22 ml) angelica root (*Angelica archangelica*) (for attraction, healing, sweetness)
- 1 tablespoon (15 ml) chamomile (*Matricaria recutita*) (for healing)
- 1 tablespoon (15 ml) lavender (*Lavandula officinalis*) (for healing, peace, relaxation)
- ½ tablespoon (7 ml) spearmint (*Mentha spicata*) (for healing, health, relaxation, wellness)

Sweet Healing Poppet Spell

This healing poppet uses Sweet Healing Powder and Blue Witches' Salt #2 to target specific areas of the body in need of healing.

Materials

- 2 6 × 6-inch (15 × 15-cm) squares of blue fabric
- Pen or marker
- Scissors
- Needle
- Dark blue thread
- Blue Witches' Salt #2
- Poly-fil, optional
- 3 needles
- Sweet Healing Powder

Working

1. Place the two pieces of blue fabric on top of each other. Use the pen or marker to draw out a human shape on the top piece.
2. Use the scissors to cut out the human shape, cutting through both pieces of fabric.
3. Thread the needle and tie a knot at the end to secure the thread.
4. Begin to stitch up the poppet. Use a simple over-and-under stitch. You want to leave an opening to fill the poppet, typically the head and neck area are used for this. As you stitch the poppet, chant:

    Healing energy on this day, in this vessel you shall stay.

5. Begin to fill the poppet's body using the witches' salt. If you are using Poly-fil to create a poofy and plush poppet, alternate between adding salt and Poly-fil so that the materials are combined and distributed evenly throughout the poppet.
6. Once the poppet is full, finish stitching it closed.
7. Hold the poppet and inhale deeply. Exhale over the poppet. With your exhale, state:

   "Poppet, I name thee (name of the individual who needs healing)."

8. Stab each pin into the area of the body that needs healing (so chest for lung and heart issues, stomach for intestinal issues, etc.). As you stab the pins, state:

   "I cast this healing spell so that (name of individual) may be well."

9. Sprinkle the Sweet Healing Powder over the pins. Repeat the statement from step 8.
10. Once a day while the target needs healing, carefully rub some of the Sweet Healing Powder over the pins.
11. When the healing has finished, cleanse the poppet by covering it with salt or burying it in the earth (or the soil of a potted plant) for twenty-four hours. The poppet can then be used to heal another individual.

Cocoa Depression Relief Healing Powder

Healing depression takes a lot of effort, as it is an illness that harms the mind, body, and spirit. This powder helps alleviate symptoms, allowing you to move forward with your life.

MATERIALS

- 1 cup (250 ml) cocoa powder (*Theobroma cacao*) (for depression relief, happiness, mood stabilization)
- 2½ tablespoons (37 ml) Saint-John's-wort (*Hypericum perforatum*) (for depression relief)
- 2 tablespoons (30 ml) lavender (*Lavandula officinalis*) (for depression relief, healing, health, wellness)
- ½ tablespoon (7 ml) passionflower (*Passiflora incarnata*) (for depression relief, healing, health, wellness)

To Bring Cheer & Lift the Mood Spell

This spell works great when you need to help cheer someone up. Use it to raise the vibrations and lift their mood.

MATERIALS

- Small plate
- Fashion doll with a removable head
- Taper candleholder

- Yellow taper candle
- Lighter or matches
- Cocoa Depression Relief Healing Powder
- Pin, needle, or knife

WORKING

1. Prepare your workspace by setting the plate behind the candleholder.
2. Hold the doll in your hand. State:

   Doll, I name thee (name of individual in need of depression relief). From their depression set them free.

3. Remove the head from the fashion doll and fill the head with powder. State:

   A better mood for (name of individual who needs relief).

4. Once the head is full, return the head to the body and place the doll on the plate sitting up.
5. Use the pin, needle, or knife to carve the word "Happiness" or "Cheer" on two sides of the candle.
6. Set the candle in the holder.
7. Light the candle. As you do so, state:

   By this candlelight, a lighter mood from this rite.

8. Let the candle burn for ten to fifteen minutes, then extinguish the candle.

9. Once a day, until the candle has completely burned, repeat steps 7 and 8.
10. When the candle has burned down, remove the doll head and dispose of the powder and candle remains.

Wellness Powder

This is a great powder for a general boost to health and wellness. The sweetness in this powder comes from lavender and spearmint, which are both well known for their healing properties.

MATERIALS

- ¼ cup (90 ml) lavender (*Lavandula officinalis*) (for healing, peace, wellness)
- ¼ cup (90 ml) spearmint (*Mentha spicata*) (for healing, mental focus, wellness)
- 2 tablespoons (30 ml) catnip (*Nepeta cataria*) (for happiness, health, wellness)
- 1 tablespoon (15 ml) allheal (*Prunella vulgaris*) (for healing)
- 1 tablespoon (15 ml) marigold (*Calendula officinalis*) (for healing, health, wellness)

Love & Lust Powders

These sweetening powders can be used in workings or by themselves to attract love into your life. Sugar is used in love powders to reflect the sweetness that comes from feelings of affection, infatuation, and passion.

Romantic Partnership Powder

This powder works great to attract your ideal partner, one who will love and cherish you.

MATERIALS

- 1 cup (250 ml) sugar (*Saccharum officinarum*) (for attraction, love, sweetness)
- 1 tablespoon (15 ml) cedar (*Cedrus libani*) (for healing)
- 1 tablespoon (15 ml) jasmine (*Jasminum grandiflorum*) (for love, relationships, romance)
- 1 tablespoon (15 ml) lovage (*Levisticum officinale*) (for love, relationships, romance)
- 1 tablespoon (15 ml) pine needles (*Pinus* spp.) (for healing, health, wellness)
- 1 tablespoon (15 ml) red rose petals (*Rosa rubiginosa*) (for love, relationships, romance)

Lust Grow Between Us Powder

This powder is for when you feel that the spark of lust and desire between you and your partner has faded. This powder works best when the relationship is still healthy and strong but the level of sexual desire has sunk lower than you would like.

MATERIALS

- ¾ cup (180 ml) sugar (*Saccharum officinarum*) (for attraction, desire, sweetness)
- 2 tablespoons (30 ml) coriander seeds (*Coriandrum sativum*) (for lust)

- 1 tablespoon (15 ml) dill seeds (*Anethum graveolens*) (for lust)
- ½ tablespoon (7 ml) ginger (*Zingiber officinale*) (for heat, lust, passion)
- ½ tablespoon (7 ml) lemongrass (*Cymbopogon citratus*) (for lust)

Increase Passion & Desire Powder

Sometimes the sparks of lust and desire can fade in long-term relationships. Use this powder to help open your partner to your needs and the exploration of new sexual and intimate experiences.

MATERIALS

- ½ cup (125 ml) sugar (*Saccharum officinarum*) (for attraction, desire, enjoyment)
- ½ cup (125 ml) cocoa powder (*Theobroma cacao*) (for attraction, desire, lust, passion)
- 1½ tablespoons (22 ml) cayenne pepper (*Capsicum annuum*) (for desire, lust, passion, sexuality)
- 1 tablespoon (15 ml) cinnamon (*Cinnamomum verum*) (for love, lust, relationships, romance, sweetness)
- ½ tablespoon (7 ml) dill (*Anethum graveolens*) (for desire, lust, passion, sexuality)

Increase Passion & Desire Charm Bag

Sometimes when people have been in long-term relationships, it can feel like the passion between partners is diminishing. Use this charm bag to pump up and reinvigorate the lust and desire in your relationship.

MATERIALS

- Red drawstring charm bag
- Personal effects from you and your partner (Locks of hair work best.)
- ½ cup (125 ml) Increase Passion and Desire Powder
- Carnelian tumble (for desire, love, passion, romance, sex)

WORKING

1. Open the drawstring bag and place the personal effects inside.
2. Sprinkle a little Increase Passion and Desire Powder into the bag. As you sprinkle the first pinch of the powder, state:

   To raise passion's fire much higher.

3. Place the carnelian tumble in the bag, stating:

   Stone of carnelian, on this day, send lustful desires our way.

4. Repeat step 2.

5. Pull the drawstring bag closed. Hold the bag with your dominant hand and begin to play with it. As you play with and fondle the bag, imagine the lust and passion between you and your partner growing stronger with new, intense experiences.
6. Place the charm bag under the mattress of your bed. For one week, every night before you go to bed, rub a bit of the powder into the charm bag to feed it and keep the charm activated. After the first week, the bag only needs to be fed once a week to stay active.
7. Continue to feed the charm bag weekly until you feel the passion and desire have reignited to a point where you are satisfied. Once you are satisfied, dispose of any remaining powder and the powder in the charm bag. The bag and crystal can be cleansed and used in future magical works.

Friendship and Social Life Powders

Friendship is one of the most special relationships out there. Some people have difficulty making friends. These powders can help you attract new people into your life who may be open to being friends with you.

Increase Popularity Powder

The primary goal of this powder is to have more people want to spend time with you.

MATERIALS

- ¾ cup (180 ml) sugar (*Saccharum officinarum*) (for attraction, relationships, sweetness)
- 1½ tablespoons (22 ml) pennyroyal (*Mentha pulegium*) (for friendship, people, relationships, socialization)
- 1 tablespoon (15 ml) catnip (*Nepeta cataria*) (for friendship, happiness)
- 1 tablespoon (15 ml) pink rose petals (*Rosa rubiginosa*) (for friendship, love)
- ½ tablespoon (7 ml) rosemary (*Salvia rosmarinus*) (for communication, love, open hearts, to open the mind)

Friendship Powder

Use this powder when you want to open yourself up to meet people and make new friends. For best results, use this powder in the creation of a charm to attract friends to you.

MATERIALS

- 1 cup (250 ml) sugar (*Saccharum officinarum*) (for attraction, sweetness)
- 2½ tablespoons (37 ml) magnetic sand (for attraction)
- 1 tablespoon (15 ml) catnip (*Nepeta cataria*) (for friendship, happiness, joy)
- 1 tablespoon (15 ml) pink rose petals (*Rosa rubiginosa*) (for friendship, gentle love)
- ½ tablespoon (7 ml) passionflower (*Passiflora incarnata*) (for friendship)

Bring In New Friends Candle Spell

Friends are wonderful people to have in our lives. Sometimes you can drift apart from friends you've had for a long time. Other times you may just want to meet new people who share an interest with you. Use this spell to bring life to old friendships and introduce new friends into your life.

MATERIALS

- Small plate
- Ground clove (*Syzygium aromaticum*) (for friendship, relationships)
- Friendship Powder
- Pink taper candle
- Pin, needle, or knife
- Taper candleholder
- Lighter or matches

WORKING

1. Set the plate in the center of your working area.
2. Sprinkle the ground clove in a line going in a clockwise fashion from the center of the plate to the edge. As you sprinkle the clove, state:

   Friendships sweet. New friends I'll meet.

3. Again starting at the center of the plate, sprinkle Friendship Powder in a clockwise fashion going outward. While you sprinkle the powder, state:

   To friends new who to the end are true.

4. Place the candleholder in the center of the plate.
5. Use the pin, needle, or knife to carve the words "New Friendship" on two sides of the candle.
6. Light the candle. As you do so, state:

   By this candle, burning bright, strong new friendships that are tight come my way on this night.

7. Let the candle burn for ten to fifteen minutes. As the candle burns, think about the kind of friends you want to have and the type of people you like to be around. Direct those images and feelings into the candle.
8. Extinguish the candle.
9. Every day, until the candle has been completely burned, repeat steps 6 through 8. While you are burning the candle, if you feel the desire to go somewhere or do something, take note of that inspiration. It is spirit telling you where you'll find your new friends.
10. Continue to repeat steps 6 through 9 until you are certain that any new friendships are going to be strong and last a long time.
11. With new friendships manifested and going strongly, you can now thank the herbs for their help in gaining new friends. Dispose of the herbal materials and candle remains in the trash.

Socialize Me Powder

It can be difficult to meet new people at times. This powder makes it easier for you to open up to other people—and for other people to be open to you and your personality.

MATERIALS

- ¾ cup (180 ml) sugar (*Saccharum officinarum*) (for attraction, relationships, sweetness)
- 2 tablespoons (30 ml) pennyroyal (*Mentha pulegium*) (for friendship, socialization, to attract people)
- 1 tablespoon (15 ml) passionflower (*Passiflora incarnata*) (for friendship, love, relationships)
- 1 tablespoon (15 ml) rosemary (*Salvia rosmarinus*) (for confidence, open minds, peace)
- 1 teaspoon (5 ml) bar or nightclub dirt (for people, socialization)

Luck Powders

Luck is an important part of our lives. When small or trivial things keep going wrong, it is often said we have bad luck. When everything seems to fall into place without any problems, we say we have a streak of good luck. Use these magical powders to help change your bad luck into better luck.

Lucky Day, Happy Day Powder

Good luck often brings feelings of happiness and joy. Use this powder to bring good luck, love, and joy into your life.

MATERIALS

- 1 cup (250 ml) sugar (*Saccharum officinarum*) (for attraction)
- 2½ tablespoons (37 ml) allspice (*Pimenta dioica*) (for friendship, good luck, love)
- 1 tablespoon (15 ml) orange zest (*Citrus sinensis*) (for cleansing, peace, to attract luck, remove bad luck)
- 1 tablespoon (15 ml) pennyroyal (*Mentha pulegium*) (for relationships, to attract good luck, remove bad luck)
- ½ tablespoon (7 ml) cramp bark (*Viburnum opulus*) (for good luck, to protect luck)

Sweeten Luck Powder

Having good luck is one of the sweetest things in the world. Mix up and use this powder to generate and sweeten good luck.

MATERIALS

- 2 cups (500 ml) sugar (*Saccharum officinarum*) (to attract good luck, sweeten luck)
- ¼ cup (60 ml) chamomile (*Matricaria recutita*) good luck

- 1 tablespoon (15 ml) orange zest (*Citrus sinensis*) (for good luck, to attract good luck, remove bad luck)
- 1 tablespoon (15 ml) rose hips (*Rosa rubiginosa*) (for luck)

Happy-Go-Lucky Powder

This powder can be used to increase your luck and bring happiness into the lives of the people around you.

MATERIALS

- 2 cups (500 ml) sugar (*Saccharum officinarum*) (for attraction, happiness, joy, sweetness)
- 2 tablespoons (30 ml) allspice (*Pimenta dioica*) (for good luck, prosperity, success)
- 2 tablespoons (30 ml) clover (*Trifolium repens*) (for good luck, happiness, peace)
- 1½ tablespoons (22 ml) meadowsweet (*Filipendula ulmaria*) (for happiness, joy, luck, to attract luck)
- ½ tablespoon (7 ml) catnip (*Nepeta cataria*) (for happiness, joy)

Attract Luck & Happiness Charm

This spell uses Happy-Go-Lucky powder to increase your good luck and bring happiness into your life.

MATERIALS

- Smiling or a sun-shaped key chain
- Small plate
- 2 magnets (to attract good luck, repel bad luck)
- Happy-Go-Lucky Powder

WORKING

1. Place the key chain in the center of the plate.
2. Set the two magnets across from each other with the plate in the center. Have both negatively charged sides facing out, or away from the plate. This will repel any ill will or bad luck sent your way and attract good luck to the charm in the center. As you place each magnet, state:

   Magnets, good luck do you attract. Bad luck shall you send back.

3. Cover the key chain with the powder, reciting the following statement three times:

   Good luck brings with it happiness and a smile. Attract good luck that will stay a while.

4. Set the plate somewhere it will not be disturbed for twenty-four to forty-eight hours. As the key chain is covered with Happy-Go-Lucky Powder, it will become infused with the energy from the powder, absorbing that good luck energy.
5. After twenty-four hours, dig out the key chain.
6. Attach the key chain to your keys and carry it around with you. As long as you are carrying

this key chain, you will attract good luck and happiness to your life.

7. Once a month, repeat steps 1 through 6 to keep the charm charged. When you no longer wish to keep this charm active, simply stop charging it.

Family & Home Powders

The final type of sweetening powder I would like to share with you is that of peaceful home powders. Conjure work has always been about the home and family. There is a large variety of spells designed to keep the family home a place of peace and love.

Peaceful, Happy & Joyful Home Powder

This powder can be used to keep your home peaceful and filled with joy. Out of all the magical powders that I've made over the years, peaceful home powders are my favorite. A home brimming with peace, happiness, and joy is a healthy home filled with love.

MATERIALS

- 1 cup (250 ml) sugar (*Saccharum officinarum*) (for happiness, joy, sweeteness)
- 2 tablespoons (30 ml) meadowsweet (*Filipendula ulmaria*) (for happiness, joy, love, peace, peace in the home)

- 1 tablespoon (15 ml) catnip (*Nepeta cataria*) (for happiness, joy)
- 1 tablespoon (15 ml) rosemary (*Salvia rosmarinus*) (for communication, healing, love, peace in the home, understanding)
- 1 tablespoon (15 ml) rose petals (*Rosa rubiginosa*) (for happiness, love)

No Jinx Peace Powder

Sometimes the cause of stress and problems in the home may come in the form of baneful magic. The following powder can be used to ensure that your home is kept peaceful by repelling all baneful magic that is sent your way.

MATERIALS

- 1 cup (250 ml) honeysuckle (*Lonicera caprifolium*) (for family, home, love, to protect love in the home, sweeten things)
- ½ cup (125 ml) peppermint (*Mentha piperita*) (for calm, cleansing, love, peace, sweetness)
- 2 tablespoons (30 ml) cumin seeds (*Cuminum cyminum*) (to deflect evil)
- 2 tablespoons (30 ml) lavender (*Lavandula officinalis*) (for calm, cleansing, peace, protection of the peace)
- 2 tablespoons (30 ml) rosemary (*Salvia rosmarinus*) (for cleansing, peaceful home, protection)

Reflective Tin House Protection Ward

This is a small protection charm that can be hidden in plain sight in your home, taking up little physical space. Any negativity and ill will that have been sent your way will be trapped and/or sent back to the one it came from.

MATERIALS

- Small metal tin
- No Jinx Peace Powder
- Kudzu (*Pueraria montana*) or any ivy or vinelike plant (to entangle evil, trap evil, trip evil)
- Gray Witches' Salt #1
- 2 mirror fragments

WORKING

1. Open the metal tin and sprinkle a layer of No Jinx Peace Powder across the bottom. As you scatter the powder, state:

   To protect the peace in this home by repelling all that would cause disharmony.

2. Lay the kudzu down on top of the No Jinx Peace Powder. As you place the plant, state:

   To entrap and trip up all evil sent this way.

3. Add the witches' salt to the tin.

4. Place the mirror fragments in the tin. State:

   To reflect back conscious and unconscious magical and psychic attacks.

5. Close the tin. Give the tin a shake to mix the contents. This will also help the mirror fragments face different sides of the tin, adding more reflection to the mix.

6. Set the tin on a shelf, table, or cabinet somewhere in the living room or main room of your home. As long as the charm remains in place, your home will be protected from any baneful magic or toxic energy directed at you or your family.

Home Sweet Home Powder

This peaceful home powder was inspired by the saying "home sweet home." Use this powder to keep communication open between members of the household and to promote a sweet and peaceful loving home.

MATERIALS

- ¾ cup (180 ml) sugar (*Saccharum officinarum*) (to sweeten)
- ¼ cup (60 ml) lavender (*Lavandula officinalis*) (for calm, cleansing, cooling, love, peace)
- 2 tablespoons (30 ml) peppermint (*Mentha piperita*) (for healing, calm, cooling, peace)

- 1 tablespoon (15 ml) honeysuckle (*Lonicera caprifolium*) (to protect the love and peace of the home)
- 1 tablespoon (15 ml) rosemary (*Salvia rosmarinus*) (for communication, peace in the home, understanding)

Floor Sweeps

One of the more unique practices I learned about through my Conjure training was the use of herbal floor sweeps. I was taught how brooms can be used to remove as well as invite in. Floor sweeps are a very old and traditional form of Conjure magic.

These powders are typically laid down on the floor for a week and swept up as part of the disposal. At other times, the powder is distributed through an area by being swept into the room. Along with brooms, brushes and feather dusters can also be used to distribute these powders. One of the alternative names for *magical powders* is *dusting powders*. Magical floor sweeps are the perfect illustration of this concept. Note that in carpeted homes or other areas where vacuums are preferred, you can simply use a vacuum to dispose of the powder rather than a broom.

Repelling Evil & Toxic People Powders

The following floor sweeps are used to repel unwanted individuals from your home. This applies to all sorts of people, from family members to those you just met. Only individuals whose behaviors and attitudes are toxic will be affected. Anyone else will still be able to come and go as freely as you wish.

Don't Come Again Sweep

Sometimes we have company over, and we decide we do not wish to have them enter our home again. This sweep works to keep those individuals from coming back.

MATERIALS

- ½ cup (125 ml) salt (to neutralize energy)
- ¼ cup (60 ml) ground black peppercorns (*Piper nigrum*) (for protection, removal)
- 2 tablespoons (30 ml) pine needles (*Pinus* spp.) (for cleansing, protection, removal)
- 1 tablespoon (15 ml) rosemary (*Salvia rosmarinus*) (for cleansing, healthy home, removal)

Toxic Individuals Be Gone Sweep

Cutting toxic individuals from our lives can be a difficult thing to do. Use this sweep after toxic individuals leave to encourage them to stay away and out of your life.

MATERIALS

- ½ cup (125 ml) sea salt (for banishment, cleansing, removal, to neutralize evil)
- 10 cat's eye shells (for protection, removal, reversal)
- 2 tablespoons (30 ml) rosemary (*Salvia rosmarinus*) (for cleansing, healthy home, removal)
- 1 tablespoon (15 ml) galangal root (*Alpinia galanga*) (for banishment, removal, reversal)

Toxic Family/Friend Cut & Clear Working

Sometimes there are people who—despite having been in our lives for a long time—end up being toxic to us. Use this spell to remove those individuals from your life.

MATERIALS

- Pin, needle, or knife
- White taper candle
- Taper candleholder
- Dustpan
- Toxic Individuals Be Gone Sweep
- Lighter or matches
- Small broom

WORKING

1. Use the pin, needle, or knife to carve the name of the toxic individual into two sides of the candle.
2. Place the candleholder in the dustpan. Set the candle in the holder.
3. Fill the dustpan with Toxic Individuals Be Gone Sweep.
4. Light the candle. As you do so, state:

   As this candle does burn bright, an end to this toxic relationship is in sight.

5. Let the candle burn for ten to fifteen minutes, then extinguish the candle.
6. Once a day, until the candle has completely burned, light the candle for ten minutes. As you light the candle, repeat the statement from step 4.
7. When the candle has finished burning, let the wax remnants cool and remove the candle and holder from the dustpan.
8. Using the broom, sweep the Toxic Individuals Be Gone Sweep across every door and window in your home. Dispose of any remaining powder and the candle wax.

Bind & Repel Sweep

This sweep works to bind those who have caused you harm, preventing them from hurting anyone else. This sweep also returns all their negative actions to them.

MATERIALS

- ½ cup (125 ml) marjoram (*Origanum majorana*) (to repel evil, repel toxic individuals)
- ½ cup (125 ml) thyme (*Thymus vulgaris*) (for protection, removal, to repel evil)
- 2 tablespoons (30 ml) devil's shoestring (*Viburnum alnifolium*) (for binding, to entangle evil, repel evil)
- 1 tablespoon (15 ml) ivy (*Hedera helix*) (for binding, protection, trapping)
- 1 tablespoon (15 ml) kudzu (*Pueraria montana*) (for binding, protection, trapping)

Cleansing & Removal Sweeps

The sweeps in the previous section work by targeting specific forces and individuals and keeping them away from you. These cleansing and removal sweeps work to remove energies already present.

Cinnamon Cleansing Sweep

Cinnamon and salt work well together to neutralize baneful energy and transform it into useful, blessed energy.

MATERIALS

- ½ cup (125 ml) ground cinnamon (*Cinnamomum verum*) (for blessing, cleansing)
- ¼ cup (60 ml) sea salt (for cleansing, removal, to neutralize)

- 2 tablespoons (30 ml) rosemary (*Salvia rosmarinus*) (for protection, purification, removal)
- 1 tablespoon (15 ml) black peppercorns (*Piper nigrum*) (for cleansing, removal, reversal)

Miasma Removal Sweep

Miasma is a term for bad air. After difficult discussions in the home, there is tension and miasma could develop. Use this sweep to cleanse your home when there is tension.

MATERIALS

- ¾ cup (180 ml) parsley (*Petroselinum crispum*) (for cleansing, protection against unwanted energy, to repel miasma)
- 1 tablespoon (15 ml) oregano (*Origanum vulgare*) (for cleansing, protection)
- 1 tablespoon (15 ml) pine needles (*Pinus* spp.) (for cleansing, protection, removal)
- 1 tablespoon (15 ml) rosemary (*Salvia rosmarinus*) (for cleansing, peace in the home, removal)

Heavy-Duty Cleansing Sweep & Wash

Coffee (*Coffea arabica*) and hyssop (*Hyssopus officinalis*) are two of the most powerful cleansing herbs available. This sweep uses their power to clear your home when it feels like the energy is being weighed down. To use this sweep as a wash, simply place the powder in cheesecloth or a muslin drawstring bag, then add to water.

MATERIALS

- ½ cup (125 ml) ground coffee (*Coffea arabica*) (for cleansing, removal)
- ¼ cup (60 ml) hyssop (*Hyssopus officinalis*) (for cleansing, hex breaking, removal, reversal)
- 1 tablespoon (15 ml) basil (*Ocimum basilicum*) (for cleansing, exorcisms, protection, removal)
- 1 tablespoon (15 ml) cedar (*Cedrus libani*) (for cleansing, protection, removal)
- 1 tablespoon (15 ml) pine needles (*Pinus* spp.) (for cleansing, protection, removal)

High-Powered Exorcism & Protection Spell

This spell uses the Heavy-Duty Cleansing Sweep and Wash to remove any malicious spirit, baneful magic, or bad luck from your home, preventing those forces from impacting your life.

MATERIALS

- Heavy-Duty Cleansing Sweep and Wash
- Small mason jar with lid
- 70-to-120-proof alcohol (You can use rubbing alcohol if other alcohol is not available.)
- Cheesecloth
- Twine or elastic band
- Spray bottle
- Spring or tap water

- Pen
- Label sticker
- Cleaning rags
- Small pin, needle, or nail for each room of your home (for protection)
- Gray Witches' Salt #3

WORKING

1. Pour the Heavy-Duty Cleansing Sweep and Wash into the mason jar.
2. Fill the jar with alcohol, covering the powder.
3. Seal the jar and shake it vigorously to mix the powder and alcohol together.
4. Set the jar in a cool, dark place for one week. During this week, shake the jar two times a day to keep mixing the contents.
5. After one week, place the cheesecloth over the mouth of the mason jar. Use twine or elastic to secure the cheesecloth. Pour the mix from the jar into the spray bottle, straining it.
6. Fill any remaining space in the spray bottle with spring or tap water. Seal the spray bottle and shake it to mix the contents together.
7. Label the bottle "Heavy-Duty Cleansing Spray."
8. One room at a time, spray down each wall in your home and use the cleaning rags to wipe it down. As you cleanse each wall, recite Psalm 23:

The Lord is my shepherd, I lack nothing.
He makes me lie down in green pastures,
he leads me beside quiet waters,
he refreshes my soul.
He guides me along the right paths
for his name's sake.
Even though I walk
through the darkest valley,
I will fear no evil,
for you are with me;
your rod and your staff,
they comfort me.
You prepare a table before me
in the presence of my enemies.
You anoint my head with oil;
my cup overflows.
Surely your goodness and love will follow me
all the days of my life,
and I will dwell in the house of the Lord
forever.[5]

9. Hide a pin, needle, or nail safely in each room.
10. Cover the pin, needle, or nail with Gray Witches' Salt #3. As you do so, state:

    Sharp object today, shred and destroy baneful energy sent this way. Return the energy back to its home or get lost forever to roam.

11. Store the remaining spray somewhere dark, dry, and away from direct heat. Left in those conditions, the spray has a shelf life of six months to

5. Psalm 23.

a year. To keep the house cleansed, repeat steps 8 through 10 every six to eight weeks. Create a new batch of wash as needed.

Money, Luck & Prosperity Sweeps

Money, luck, and prosperity are all things that everyone seeks. Use these magical sweeps to brush and bring money, luck, and prosperity into your home or place of business.

Attract Customers & Sales Sweep

Customers and sales are the life blood of businesses. Use this sweep daily to attract customers and sales to your place of business.

MATERIALS

- ¼ cup (60 ml) fumitory (*Fumaria officinalis*) (for money, sales, success, to attract customers)
- ¼ cup (60 ml) pine needles (*Pinus* spp.) (for fertility, money, prosperity, success, wealth)
- 1 tablespoon (15 ml) yellow dock (*Rumex crispus*) (to attract money)
- ½ tablespoon (7 ml) fenugreek (*Trigonella foenum-graecum*) (for money, prosperity, sales, success)
- ½ tablespoon (7 ml) nutmeg (*Myristica fragrans*) (for attraction, good luck, money, sales, success)

Sweet Success Sweep

Use this mixture to bring success every day your business or place of work is open. It can be used effectively in retail environments as well as in service offices.

MATERIALS

- ½ cup (125 ml) sugar (*Saccharum officinarum*) (for attraction)
- ½ cup (125 ml) orange zest (*Citrus sinensis*) (for luck, money, success)
- 2 tablespoons (30 ml) allspice (*Pimenta dioica*) (for money, prosperity, success)
- 1 tablespoon (15 ml) pine needles (*Pinus* spp.) (for money, wealth, success)
- 1 tablespoon (15 ml) yellow dock (*Rumex crispus*) (for money, sales, to attract sales)

Sweet, Successful Sales Daily Working

Use this spell to bring excellent sales into your business. If possible, this spell should be performed daily for maximum effectiveness.

MATERIALS

- Small bowl
- 1 cup (250 ml) baby powder
- ½ cup (125 ml) Sweet Success Sweep
- ½ cup (125 ml) Green Witches' Salt #2
- Spoon or wand

- Old spice jar
- Pen
- Label sticker
- Broom

WORKING

1. In the bowl, mix the baby powder, Sweet Success Sweep, and witches' salt together. While you stir the mixture, repeat Psalm 90:17 five to seven times, or until all the materials are thoroughly blended:

    May the favor of the Lord our God rest on us;
    establish the work of our hands for us—
    yes, establish the work of our hands.[6]

2. Using the spoon or wand, place the mixture in the jar for storage. Label the mixture "Sweet and Salty Successful Sales."
3. At the start of each business day, sprinkle the mixture along the walls of your business and across a path from the door to the register or your sales desk or office. Recite Psalm 90:17 while you sprinkle the powder.
4. At the end of the day, sweep up the mixture. Dispose of the gathered powder at a crossroads or intersection near your place of work.

6. Psalm 90:17.

Victory & Luck Sweep

When things go our way and we overcome problems, achievements make us feel lucky. This sweep brings victory over obstacles standing in the way of your success. You will also find better luck and prosperity in your life with this sweep.

MATERIALS

- 1½ cups (375 ml) magnetic sand (for attraction)
- 2 tablespoons (30 ml) allspice (*Pimenta dioica*) (for good luck, money, prosperity, success, wealth)
- 2 tablespoons (30 ml) woodruff (*Galium odoratum*) (for prosperity, success, victory)
- 1 tablespoon (15 ml) alum (for good luck)
- 1 tablespoon (15 ml) clover (*Trifolium repens*) (for good luck)

Love & Relationship Sweeps

The following floor sweeps can be used to help bring in many forms of love. From romantic love to friendship and self-love, these powders can be useful in any type of love magic you perform.

Open to Love Sweep

This sweep is designed to be used in magic for inviting love into your life in general. When working with this sweep, you may find romance, friendship, companionship, or even the love of an animal.

MATERIALS

- ½ cup (125 ml) lemon balm (*Melissa officinalis*) (for block busting, general love, relationships, to attract love, road opens)
- ½ cup (125 ml) rose petals (*Rosa rubiginosa*) (for love, relationships, romance)
- 1½ tablespoons (22 ml) catnip (*Nepeta cataria*) (for happiness, love, love from animals)
- 1½ tablespoons (22 ml) clove (*Syzygium aromaticum*) (for love, relationships, sweetness)
- 1 tablespoon (15 ml) jasmine (*Jasminum grandiflorum*) (for friendship, love, love of family)

Citrus Love Sweep

Citrus fruits are both sweet and sour. Use this powder to bring a love into your life that is strong enough to handle the good, or sweet, with the bad, or sour.

MATERIALS

- ½ cup (125 ml) lemon zest (*Citrus limon*) (for love, sourness)
- ½ cup (125 ml) orange zest (*Citrus sinensis*) (for attraction, love, relationships, sweetness)
- 2 tablespoons (30 ml) lemon balm (*Melissa officinalis*) (for love, relationships, to attract love)
- 1 tablespoon (15 ml) cinnamon (*Cinnamomum verum*) (for attraction, love, relationships, sexuality, sweetness)
- 1 tablespoon (15 ml) lavender (*Lavandula officinalis*) (for attraction, love, peace, relationships, sweetness)

Romance & Love Sweep

This magical sweep can be used to keep your romance fresh and the love between you and a partner alive.

MATERIALS

- ½ cup (125 ml) baby powder (for attraction, healing, love)
- ¼ cup (60 ml) red rose petals (*Rosa rubiginosa*) (for love, relationships, romance)
- 1 tablespoon (15 ml) jasmine (*Jasminum grandiflorum*) (for love, relationships, romance)
- 1 tablespoon (15 ml) lovage (*Levisticum officinale*) (for love, relationships, romance)
- 1 tablespoon (15 ml) yellow dock (*Rumex crispus*) (for love, relationships, to attract love)

To Keep Love Fresh Spell

This spell uses both the Citrus Love Sweep and the Romance and Love Sweep to renew and strengthen the feelings of love that exist between you and a partner.

MATERIALS

- Dustpan
- ½ cup (125 ml) Citrus Love Sweep
- ½ cup (125 ml) Romance and Love Sweep
- Small broom

WORKING

1. In the dustpan, combine the Citrus Love Sweep and the Romance and Love Sweep, using the broom to stir them together. While you combine the blends, repeat the following chant seven to nine times:

    Love refreshed and renewed stays strong and true.

2. Once the two sweeps are combined, take the dustpan to the center of your living room and use the broom to sweep the mixture from the center of the room out to its edges.
3. Repeat in each room of your home.
4. After twenty-four hours, sweep up the mixture and sprinkle it around the outside of your home, stating:

    May the hearts of those in this home be filled with love, light, and plenty of delight.

5. Repeat once a month if you feel the love has grown stale. Otherwise perform this working once a year, ideally around an anniversary, for love and devotion.

Peaceful Home Sweeps

Peaceful home sweeps are great tools to keep your home feeling harmonious and full of love and life. A peaceful home is a happy and healthy home, and everyone deserves to live in such a place. These sweeps provide a subtle way to work peaceful home magic without the work being an overtly open spell.

Cool Peace-Loving Home Sweep

Use this sweep to keep calm, cool heads in your home, allowing for clear communication between everyone living there.

MATERIALS

- ½ cup (125 ml) peppermint (*Mentha piperita*) (for calmness, cleansing, love, peace)
- 2 tablespoons (30 ml) rosemary (*Salvia rosmarinus*) (for cleansing, peace in the home, open communication, to open the mind)
- 1 tablespoon (7 ml) pennyroyal (*Mentha pulegium*) (for joy, love, peace, peace in the home)
- 1 tablespoon (7 ml) passionflower (*Passiflora incarnata*) (for friendship, love, peace)

Stress-Be-Gone Sweep

Stress can cause many issues in the home. Use this sweep to remove any stress and anxiety that may be bringing about difficulties.

MATERIALS

- ¾ cup (180 ml) lavender (*Lavandula officinalis*) (for anxiety relief, calm, cleansing, love, peace, protection, stress relief)

- 1 tablespoon (15 ml) chamomile (*Matricaria recutita*) (for anxiety relief, calm, cleansing, healing, peace, stress relief)
- 1 tablespoon (15 ml) lemon balm (*Melissa officinalis*) (for anxiety relief, cleansing, love, peace)
- 1 tablespoon (15 ml) peppermint (*Mentha piperita*) (for anxiety relief, calm, cleansing, healing, peace, stress relief)

Peace & Love Sweep

Peace and love are connected. Use this sweep to bring both peace and love into your home.

MATERIALS

- 1 cup (250 ml) rosemary (*Salvia rosmarinus*) (for cleansing, communication, love, peace in the home, protection)
- 1½ tablespoons (22 ml) chervil (*Anthriscus cerefolium*) (for joy, peace)
- 1 tablespoon (15 ml) lavender (*Lavandula officinalis*) (for cleansing, love, peace, protection)
- 1 tablespoon (15 ml) rose petals (*Rosa rubiginosa*) (for love, protection of those you love)
- ½ tablespoon (7 ml) lemon balm (*Melissa officinalis*) (for anxiety relief, cleansing, love, peace)

Peace & Love in the Home Candle Spell

This spell combines the soft serenity that comes from using the Peace and Love Sweep with the gentle glow of candlelight to invite a sense of harmony, calm, and love into your home.

MATERIALS

- Dustpan
- Peace and Love Sweep
- Pink pillar candle (A glass-encased candle works best.)
- Lighter or matches
- Small broom

WORKING

1. In the center of the dustpan, place the candle.
2. Pour the Peace and Love Sweep around the base of the candle, filling the dustpan with the powder.
3. Light the candle.
4. Carefully carry the dustpan and candle to each room of your home.
5. As you walk through each room, use the small broom to sprinkle a bit of the powder in each one. As you scatter the sweep, state:

   With this candle's soft glow, peace in this home all will know.

6. After twenty-four hours, clean up the sweep and dispose of it at the end of your driveway or parking lot.
7. Repeat the spell once a month as needed to bring continued peace and love into your home.

Protection Sweeps

Protection sweeps work best when they are used after a cleansing working. By using a protection sweep directly after cleansing work, you are better able to defend yourself from that which you just removed.

Strength & Power Protective Sweep

Use this sweep to bring out your strength and power to create an energetic shield that protects your home from unwanted individuals and forces.

MATERIALS

- ¾ cup (180 ml) pine needles (*Pinus* spp.) (for cleansing, protection, removal)
- 1½ tablespoons (22 ml) woodruff (*Galium odoratum*) (for power, protection, strength)
- 1 tablespoon (15 ml) red brick dust (for protection, strength)
- ½ tablespoon (7 ml) juniper (*Juniperus communis*) (for exorcisms, protection)
- 6 acorn tops (*Quercus* spp.) (for power, protection, strength)

Ward Against Evil Sweep

This sweep will ward your home against the evil eye and other curses. Any ill will directed at you or your loved ones will be dissolved, neutralized, or reflected back at its sender.

MATERIALS

- 1 cup (250 ml) sea salt (to neutralize evil)
- 1 tablespoon (15 ml) cumin (*Cuminum cyminum*) (to deflect evil)
- 1 tablespoon (15 ml) elderflower (*Sambucus nigra*) (for cleansing, protection against baneful magic)
- 1 tablespoon (15 ml) fennel seeds (*Foeniculum vulgare*) (for cleansing, protection, to ward against evil)
- 1 tablespoon (15 ml) juniper (*Juniperus communis*) (for cleansing, protection)

Warding Evil Protection Spell

Use this working to protect yourself from the evil eye and other baneful magic. For best results, perform the spell once a month, after a monthly cleansing ritual.

MATERIALS

- Ward Against Evil Sweep
- Dustpan
- Tea light candleholder
- Black tea light candle
- Lighter or matches
- Broom

WORKING

1. Pour the sweep into the dustpan.
2. In the center of the sweep, dig a hole to place the candleholder. Set the candleholder in the hole you created and place the candle in the holder.

3. Light the candle. As you do so, recite Psalm 140:1–11:

   Rescue me, Lord, from evildoers;
   protect me from the violent,
   who devise evil plans in their hearts
   and stir up war every day.
   They make their tongues as sharp as a serpent's;
   the poison of vipers is on their lips.
   Keep me safe, Lord, from the hands of the wicked;
   protect me from the violent,
   who devise ways to trip my feet.
   The arrogant have hidden a snare for me;
   they have spread out the cords of their net
   and have set traps for me along my path.
   I say to the Lord, "You are my God."
   Hear, Lord, my cry for mercy.
   Sovereign Lord, my strong deliverer,
   you shield my head in the day of battle.
   Do not grant the wicked their desires, Lord;
   do not let their plans succeed.
   Those who surround me proudly rear their heads;
   may the mischief of their lips engulf them.
   May burning coals fall on them;
   may they be thrown into the fire,
   into miry pits, never to rise.
   May slanderers not be established in the land;
   may disaster hunt down the violent.[7]

7. Psalm 140:1–11.

4. Extinguish the candle. Remove the candle and its holder from the dustpan.
5. Place the dustpan in the center of the floor of a main room, such as your kitchen or living room. Use the broom to sweep and disperse the powder across your home. As you sweep the mixture across your floors, make sure some gets into every room and along each wall. For those with rugs or who use vacuums, take the dustpan and sprinkle the powder across your floors. Leave the sweep on the floors for twenty-four hours to set the magic.
6. After twenty-four hours, sweep up the mixture into the dustpan once again. Once you have swept everything up, take the sweep outside and sprinkle it along the outside walls of your home. This secures your home inside and out.

Subtle Shield Protective Sweep

This sweep is designed to create a strong but subtle shield of energy to protect your home or place of business. As an added bonus, one of the herbs used in this sweep has magical lore of being used to prevent theft.

MATERIALS

- ¾ cup (180 ml) sea salt (for protection, to neutralize negativity)

- 1 tablespoon (15 ml) benzoin gum (*Styrax paralleloneurus*) (for protection against theft)
- 1 tablespoon (15 ml) cascarilla powder (for protection)
- ½ tablespoon (7 ml) kudzu (*Pueraria montana*) (to entangle evil)
- ½ tablespoon (7 ml) stinging nettle leaves (*Urtica dioica*) (to repel evil, return evil to sender)

Hex & Curse Breaking Sweeps

These cleansing sweeps focus on breaking hexes or curses. Any baneful magic that has been sent to you will be dissolved and destroyed through the use of these powerful sweeps.

Angelic Hex Breaker Sweep

This house sweep calls on the power of angels using angelica root (*Angelica archangelica*) to remove hexes from your life.

MATERIALS

- ¾ cup (180 ml) angelica root (*Angelica archangelica*) (for hex breaking, protection, removal)
- 1 tablespoon (15 ml) basil (*Ocimum basilicum*) (for cleansing, removal)
- 1 tablespoon (15 ml) dill seeds (*Anethum graveolens*) (for hex breaking)
- 1 tablespoon (15 ml) wood betony (*Pedicularis canadensis*) (for cleansing, hex breaking, protection)

Super Remover Hex Breaker Sweep

This sweep uses some of the most powerful spell-breaking herbs known. Mix these materials and use this sweep when you need to remove hexes and other spells.

MATERIALS

- ½ cup (125 ml) hyssop (*Hyssopus officinalis*) (for cleansing, cutting, hex breaking, removal, spell breaking)
- 1 tablespoon (15 ml) asafetida (*Ferula assa-foetida*) (for hex breaking, protection, removal, spell breaking)
- 1 tablespoon (15 ml) rue (*Ruta graveolens*) (for hex breaking, protection, removal, spell breaking)

Coffee Hex Breaker Cleansing Sweep

Use this sweep once a week to maintain a space that has been cleansed. This cleansed area will be blessed by the sweep, protecting it from unwanted harm.

MATERIALS

- 1 cup (250 ml) coffee grounds (for cleansing, hex breaking, removal, to refresh)
- 2 tablespoons (30 ml) lemon balm (*Melissa officinalis*) (for cleansing, purification)

- 1 tablespoon (15 ml) sage (*Salvia officinalis*) (for cleansing, removal)
- 1 tablespoon (15 ml) sea salt (for cleansing, neutralization of energy, removal)

Bitter Coffee Cleansing Jinx Removal Spell

Bitter herbs such as coffee are often used in Conjure work to help cleanse oneself of hexes, curses, and jinxes. The following spell works great when you believe that your household is under magical attack. You can also use it if you believe that the place you work is being targeted.

MATERIALS

- Coffee Hex Breaker Sweep
- Broom
- Dustpan
- Small container that seals

WORKING

1. Sprinkle the sweep along the walls of each room in your home. As you sprinkle the sweep, state:

    Cleanse and clean, remove that which is baneful and unseen.

2. Using the broom and starting in the room farthest from your main entrance, begin to sweep from the outer walls to the center of the room. As you sweep, you draw out the baneful and unwanted energy.

3. Sweep the pile of powder into the dustpan.
4. Repeat steps 2 and 3 for every room in your home.
5. Pour the materials you swept up into the container.
6. Head to a crossroads near your home. When it is safe to do so, dump the mixture in the center of the crossroads, then return home. If going to the center is not practical, dump the swept-up materials in the ditch at the corners of the crossroads, then return home.

Edible Magical Powders

Spice blends make excellent magical powders. These blends can be easily added to food for kitchen magic. What makes these magical powders unique is the fact that they are all made from edible materials.

I have found these magical powders work best for protection, removal, and attraction work. I commonly use spice blends as magical powders when I attend festivals as a vendor or presenter. By ingesting the magical powders, I take that energy into myself and release it throughout the day simply going about my work.

Not all of the ingredients used throughout these recipes come as a powder. Remember to grind ingredients as necessary before blending.

Money Spice Blends

The following spice blends can be added to any foods eaten during the day to increase sales, bring money, and ensure prosperity for your business and in your daily life.

Sweet Success Powder

For best results, add this powder to your breakfast, either sprinkling some on toast or adding a pinch to your coffee or tea. This will ensure and bring you success throughout your day.

MATERIALS

- ¾ cup (180 ml) cocoa powder (*Theobroma cacao*) (for attraction, sweetness)
- 1½ tablespoons (22 ml) sugar (*Saccharum officinarum*) (for attraction)
- ½ tablespoon (7 ml) allspice (*Pimenta dioica*) (for attraction, luck, money)
- ½ tablespoon (7 ml) cinnamon (*Cinnamomum verum*) (for money, luck, prosperity)
- ½ tablespoon (7 ml) nutmeg (*Myristica fragrans*) (for attraction, luck, sales)

Strawberry Success Dessert Spell

After a long day, a sweet dessert is a great way to cap things off. Eating this dessert will ensure that all the work you have done throughout the day will be successful.

MATERIALS

- Small melting pot or double boiler
- Spoon or wand
- 6 ounces (170 grams) semisweet chocolate chips
- Sweet Success Powder
- Small baking sheet
- Wax paper
- Strawberries

WORKING

1. In the small pot or double boiler, combine the chocolate and Sweet Success Powder. Heat over low. Stir frequently to ensure a smooth and thoroughly combined chocolate mixture.
2. Line the baking sheet with wax paper.
3. When the chocolate is warm and the powder has been thoroughly mixed in, dip the strawberries into the chocolate, covering them with the syrup. As you dip the strawberries into the chocolate, state:

   Like this strawberry is sweet, great success
   I shall meet.

4. Place the strawberries on the baking sheet.
5. Set the baking sheet in the fridge for at least half an hour.
6. Remove the baking sheet from the fridge. The chocolate has set, and the strawberries are now ready to eat.

7. Dispose of any remaining chocolate in the trash, and store any leftover strawberries in an airtight container. Enjoy your sweet treat.

Sweet & Sour Success Blend

Good luck and wealth can bring happiness and joy, as well as envy from others. This blend has the sweet and sour sensations that having wealth and luck can bring.

MATERIALS

- ½ cup (125 ml) freeze-dried blueberries (*Vaccinium corymbosum*) (for money, prosperity, wealth)
- ¼ cup (60 ml) freeze-dried raspberries (*Rubus idaeus* var. *strigosus*) (for money, prosperity, wealth)
- zest from 3 oranges (*Citrus sinensis*) (for money, prosperity, wealth)
- 2½ tablespoons (37 ml) cinnamon (*Cinnamomum verum*) (for luck, money, wealth)
- 1 tablespoon (15 ml) ginger (*Zingiber officinale*) (for money, prosperity, wealth)

Protect Wealth & Success Powder

When dealing with money and prosperity, it is important to have protection against loss or theft. This blend attracts wealth while safeguarding it against theft.

MATERIALS

- ¾ cup (180 ml) pine nuts (*Pinus quadrifolia*) (for fertility, growth, prosperity, success)
- 1 tablespoon (15 ml) basil (*Ocimum basilicum*) (for money, prosperity, success, to attract money)
- 1 tablespoon (15 ml) garlic powder (*Allium sativum*) (for protection against theft)
- 1 tablespoon (15 ml) ground ginger (*Zingiber officinale*) (for money, prosperity, wealth)
- 1 tablespoon (15 ml) onion powder (*Allium cepa*) (for money, prosperity, wealth)

Wealth & Success Stir-Fry Dinner Spell

Enjoying this dish is a great way to celebrate incoming wealth or a string of unexpected successes. You can also make this meal when you need a boost in wealth and prosperity.

MATERIALS

- 1 tablespoon (15 ml) peanut or sunflower oil (You can use olive or canola oil as a substitute.) (for luck, money, prosperity, success)
- Large pan or wok
- Onion, chopped (*Allium cepa*) (for money)
- Sweet bell pepper, chopped (*Capsicum annuum*) (for money, sweetness)
- ½ cup (125 ml) snow peas (*Pisum sativum* var. *macrocarpon*) (for money)
- Large carrot, chopped (*Daucus carota*) (for fertility, success)

- ¼ cup (60 ml) cashews (*Anacardium occidentale*) (for money)
- Clove garlic, minced (*Allium sativum*) (for protection from theft)
- Spoon or wand
- Protect Wealth and Success Powder
- Beef or chicken strips
- Stir-fry sauce, soy sauce, or hoisin

WORKING

1. Add the oil to the pan and heat over medium-high.
2. Add the vegetables, garlic, and cashews to the pan and cook, stirring occasionally.
3. Rub the powder over the meat you chose to cook. If you are not using any meat, add the powder to the vegetables.
4. Add the meat to the pan, turning up the heat a little bit. As the food cooks, add the stir-fry sauce to taste.
5. Once the meat and vegetables have completely cooked, serve the food and enjoy. Rice makes a wonderful side dish for this meal.

Protection Spice Blends

Protection magic is important, as it keeps spirits away and prevents baneful magic from having an impact on your life. The following spice blends protect against the evil eye, ward against spirits, and provide powerful protection against baneful magic.

Ward Against Evil Spice Blend

By eating food made with this spice rub, you will naturally produce an energetic aura that will ward off the evil eye and other forms of simple baneful magic.

MATERIALS

- ¼ cup (60 ml) black peppercorns (*Piper nigrum*) (for protection, removal, to repel evil)
- 1 tablespoon (15 ml) garlic (*Allium sativum*) (for protection against theft)
- 1 tablespoon (15 ml) rosemary (*Salvia rosmarinus*) (for protection against evil)
- 1 tablespoon (15 ml) thyme (*Thymus vulgaris*) (for protection against evil, to ward against the evil eye)

Simple Home-Warding Spell

This is a very simple spell to protect your home. For best results perform this spell once a month to ensure your home remains protected.

MATERIALS

- 2 16-ounce mason jars with lids
- ⅓ cup (80 ml) Ward Against Evil Spice Blend
- ¼ cup (60 ml) Strength and Power Protective Sweep

- 1½ tablespoons (22 ml) dragon's blood resin (*Dracaena cinnabari*)
- Obsidian tumble
- 70-to-120-proof alcohol (You can use rubbing alcohol if other alcohol is not available.)
- Cheesecloth
- Twine or elastic band
- Large mixing bowl
- Gallon distilled water
- 16-ounce spray bottle
- Label stickers
- Pen
- Cleaning rags

WORKING

1. Add the spice blend, protective sweep, dragon's blood, and tumble to the mason jar.
2. Fill the jar with alcohol, covering the materials.
3. Seal the jar and set it in a place that is dark, cool, and dry for four to six weeks.
4. Twice a day for the next four to six weeks, shake the jar vigorously to mix and charge the contents. As you shake the jar, recite Psalm 31:4–8 five times:

   Keep me free from the trap that is set for me,
   for you are my refuge.
   Into your hands I commit my spirit;
   deliver me, Lord, my faithful God.
   I hate those who cling to worthless idols;
   as for me, I trust in the Lord.

> *I will be glad and rejoice in your love,*
> *for you saw my affliction*
> *and knew the anguish of my soul.*
> *You have not given me into the hands of*
> *the enemy*
> *but have set my feet in a spacious place.*[8]

5. After four to six weeks, place the cheesecloth over the mouth of the mason jar, securing it with twine or an elastic band. Carefully strain the liquid from the mason jar into the bowl.
6. Gently pour enough distilled water into the strained liquid to cut the smell of alcohol. Use your best judgment. I have found ¼ to ⅓ of a gallon is typically required. This process dilutes the mixture, making it safe to use on your walls.
7. Fill the spray bottle with the mixture you just created. Pour any remaining liquid into the second mason jar.
8. Seal the spray bottle and the mason jar. Label them "House Warding Spray."
9. Go through each room in your home and spray the mixture onto the walls. Use the rags to rub and spread the mixture.
10. Store the remaining spray somewhere cool, dark, and dry. Left in those conditions, the mixture will last up to one and a half years.

---

8. Psalm 31:4–8.

Peppery Protection Powder

Peppers are well known for their protective properties. This blend takes some of the most common pepper flavors and creates a spicy powder to provide protection.

MATERIALS

- ¾ cup (180 ml) black peppercorns (*Piper nigrum*) (for banishment, protection, to repel evil)
- 1 tablespoon (15 ml) cayenne pepper (*Capsicum annuum*) (for protection, to repel evil)
- 1 tablespoon (15 ml) dried jalapeño pepper (*Capsicum annuum 'Jalapeño'*) (for banishment, protection, removal, to repel evil)
- 1 tablespoon (15 ml) white pepper (*Piper nigrum*) (for banishment, protection, to repel evil)

Fiery Wall of Protection Powder

Use this spice powder to create a fiery wall of protection around you and your loved ones. As with all powders, the ingredients should be ground and combined.

MATERIALS

- ¾ cup (180 ml) cayenne pepper (*Capsicum annuum*) (for protection, removal, to repel evil)
- 1 tablespoon (15 ml) black peppercorns (*Piper nigrum*) (for banishment, protection, removal, to repel evil)

- 1 tablespoon (15 ml) dried horseradish (*Cochlearia armoracia*) (for protection, removal, reversal)
- 1 tablespoon (15 ml) garlic powder (*Allium sativum*) (for banishment, protection, removal, to repel evil)
- Dried jalapeño pepper (*Capsicum annuum 'Jalapeño'*) (for banishment, fiery protection, removal, to repel evil)

Distance Candle Protection Spell

Use this working when you want to cast a protection spell over someone who lives far away from you.

MATERIALS

- Small plate
- Photo (one you don't mind losing) or personal effect of the individual you want to protect
- Pen
- Slip of paper, if a personal effect is used
- Taper candleholder
- Fiery Wall of Protection Powder
- Black or red taper candle
- Lighter or matches

WORKING

1. Set the plate in the center of your work area.
2. On the back of the photo, write the name and date of birth of the individual you wish to protect. Underneath their name and date of

birth, write out either the word "Protection" or "Protection from (insert what they need protection from)" if there is a specific thing they need safeguarding from. When a personal effect is being used instead of a photo, write the same information on a small piece of paper.

3. Place the photo on the plate face up so the image is facing the sky. If using a personal effect, place the paper with their name and date of birth on the plate first, then set the personal effect on top of the paper.
4. Place the candleholder in the center of the plate, on top of the photo or personal effect, and set the candle in the holder.
5. Sprinkle the protection powder around the candleholder's base. As you sprinkle the powder, repeat the following statement five times:

   For (name of the individual you are protecting), a fiery wall of protection starts today. Safe from all harm shall they stay.

6. Light the candle. As you do so, state:

   Fire from the candle burning this night, protect (name of individual being protected) with all your strength and might.

7. Let the candle burn for ten minutes. After ten minutes, extinguish the candle.
8. Repeat steps 5 through 7 once a day until the candle has burned out. If you feel that protection

is still needed, begin with a new candle and continue daily until the second candle has completely burned.

9. When you feel that the protection is no longer needed and the candle(s) have been burned completely, dispose of the candle remains, the photo or personal effect and paper, and the powder. The spell has done its work, and the materials can now return to the earth through the trash and rest.

Healing Spice Blends

The foods that we eat can be powerful tools when it comes to creating and maintaining a healthy body. These powders are just a few examples of magical spice blends that can be used to heal.

Rest Well Healing Powder

This powder is designed to soothe your mind and body, allowing you to rest and heal. Note that this formula, when left unground, also works well when made into a tea.

MATERIALS

- ½ cup (125 ml) peppermint (*Mentha piperita*) (for healing, peace, removal of illness)
- 2 tablespoons (30 ml) chamomile (*Matricaria recutita*) (for healing, peace, relaxation, sleep)
- 1 tablespoon (15 ml) lavender (*Lavandula officinalis*) (for healing, peace, removal, sleep)

Sleep & Heal Working

When we are sick, sleep and rest are the most important things we can do for our body to heal. For best results, perform this spell when you have an hour or more just to rest.

MATERIALS

- Teapot
- Heat pad
- Tea ball
- Rest Well Healing Powder
- Coffee mug

WORKING

1. Fill the teapot with water and begin to heat it on the pad.
2. While the water heats, fill the tea ball with the healing powder.
3. Set the tea ball in the mug. If the water in the teapot has warmed up sufficiently, begin to pour the water over the tea ball. Steep the tea.
4. While the tea steeps, hold your hands over the mug, focusing blue light through your hands and chanting the following five times:

   Restful healing tea, I ask of thee, help me to rest easily and heal freely.

5. Once the tea has steeped to your taste, remove the tea ball and slowly drink the tea to relax. When you have finished the tea, open the tea ball

and dispose of the herbal mixture in the compost or trash, then get comfortable and allow yourself to rest and relax.

Fire Cider Powder

Fire cider is a powerful herbal remedy that quickly fights off variants of the common cold and flu. This blend is also a powerful protection powder.

When you combine Fire Cider Powder with oil and either apple cider vinegar or white vinegar, you create a tasty marinade. The powder also works well when added to hearty fall foods such as soups, stews, and chili.

Materials

- ¼ cup (60 ml) dried horseradish (*Cochlearia armoracia*) (for banishment, healing, removal)
- ¼ cup (60 ml) rosemary (*Salvia rosmarinus*) (for cleansing, healing, removal)
- 2 tablespoons (30 ml) turmeric (*Curcuma longa*) (for banishment, healing, protection, removal)
- 1½ tablespoons (22 ml) black peppercorns (*Piper nigrum*) (for banishment, healing, removal)
- ½ tablespoon (7 ml) ginger (*Zingiber officinale*) (for cleansing, healing, protection, removal)
- 1 teaspoon (5 ml) garlic powder (*Allium sativum*) (for banishment, healing, removal)
- 2 dried habanero peppers (*Capsicum chinese*) (for healing, protection, removal)

Fruity Health & Wellness Boost Powder

Unlike the other two healing blends, this powder is designed to help you maintain your health and provide an occasional boost in strength to your healing. This powder works well with dessert flavors or as part of breakfast.

MATERIALS

- 1 cup (250 ml) cocoa powder (*Theobroma cacao*) (for healing, wellness)
- 1½ tablespoons (22 ml) ground dried pineapple (*Ananas comosus*) (for healing, health, wellness)
- 1 tablespoon (15 ml) allspice (*Pimenta dioica*) (for health, wellness)
- 1 tablespoon (15 ml) cinnamon (*Cinnamomum verum*) (for protection, protection of health)
- Zest from 1 orange (*Citrus sinensis*) (for healing, protection of health, wellness)

Love & Romance Powders

Many times people say their food is prepared with love. Foods can be made with these powders to bring love to you from within yourself and from the universe.

Passion & Desire Lovers' Powder

Use this herbal powder to invite passion into you and your partner's lives and love making.

MATERIALS

- ½ cup (125 ml) rosemary (*Salvia rosmarinus*) (for love, lust)
- ¼ cup (60 ml) marjoram (*Origanum majorana*) lust, (for desire, joy, love, lust, passion)
- 2 tablespoons (30 ml) onion powder (*Allium cepa*) (for desire, love)
- 1½ tablespoons (22 ml) garlic powder (*Allium sativum*) (for desire, love, passion, protection)
- ½ tablespoon (7 ml) cayenne pepper (*Capsicum annuum*) (for desire, lust, passion)

Long-Term Love & Protection Powder

This is one of my favorite spice blends to use when I want a very basic and simple flavor. This powder helps protect you from harm and your relationship from any interference. It also brings with it love from within and will attract love into your life.

MATERIALS

- ¼ cup (60 ml) oregano (*Origanum vulgare*) (for desire, love, relationships)
- ¼ cup (60 ml) basil (*Ocimum basilicum*) (for love)
- 1 tablespoon (15 ml) thyme (*Thymus vulgaris*) (for love)
- ½ tablespoon (7 ml) garlic powder (*Allium sativum*) (for desire, love, passion, protection)
- ½ tablespoon (7 ml) onion powder (*Allium cepa*) (for desire, love, protection, protection of your love)

Love Gain Pasta Dinner Spell

This spell is inspired by some Italian folk magic that I know. Many of the herbs and spices used in traditional Italian cooking have the magical correspondences of love and protection. Use this spell to ensure love is in your life and that both you and your loved one are always protected.

MATERIALS

- Two pots
- Preferred pasta (I use spaghetti or tortellini.)
- Tomato sauce (for desire, love, passion, relationships)
- Pan
- Oil
- Ground meat, optional
- Passion and Desire Lovers' Powder
- Long-Term Relationship Love and Protection Powder
- Spatula
- Strainer

WORKING

1. Fill one of the pots with water and bring to a boil.
2. In the second pot, pour the pasta sauce and set it on low or medium and heat to a simmer.
3. While the sauce warms and the water boils, add the oil to the frying pan and begin to cook the ground meat over medium-high heat.

4. Sprinkle two pinches of the Passion and Desire Lovers' Powder into the meat and the sauce to flavor them. As you add the herbal powder, state:

   Lust is what fuels love's fire. Heat my passion, bring forth desire.

5. Once the water is boiling, add the pasta with a pinch of the Long-Term Relationship Love and Protection Powder to the pot.

6. Add 2 tablespoons (30 ml) of both Long-Term Relationship Love and Protection Powder to the sauce, adding more to taste. As you stir the powder into the sauce, state:

   A long-term relationship that is true. Protect the relationship. Thick and thin will see it through.

7. Once the meat has been cooked completely, add it to the sauce. As you stir the meat clockwise, or desoil, into the sauce, repeat the following chant seven times:

   Passion and fire fuels true love's desire. Passion from love that is true will always be with you.

8. Once the pasta has been cooked, strain the pasta over the sink and add the pasta to the sauce.

9. Serve and eat to bring passion, desire, and long-lasting true love into your life. Store any leftovers as you normally would and enjoy a few meals. Each meal brings more love, desire, and passion and ensures the relationship is protected.

Sweet Love & Joy Powder

Romance and a sense of partnership are some of the sweetest feelings of love that exist in this world. This gentle powder helps to invoke that sweet love, letting you feel a deep, passionate love and sense of joy.

MATERIALS

- ¼ cup (60 ml) cocoa powder (*Theobroma cacao*) (for desire, friendship, joy, love, passion)
- ¼ cup (60 ml) sugar (*Saccharum officinarum*) (for attraction, desire, love, relationships)
- 2 tablespoons (30 ml) cinnamon (*Cinnamomum verum*) (for desire, love, lust)
- 1 tablespoon (15 ml) clove (*Syzygium aromaticum*) (for desire, love, lust, passion, relationships)
- 1 tablespoon (15 ml) allspice (*Pimenta dioica*) (for desire, love, passion, relationships)

Joyful Love Fruit Salad Spell

Sharing food with the people you care about is one of the best ways to show that you love and cherish them. The following spell is a nice, fruity treat you can serve to friends and family so that everyone may feel the love within them and around them. This sweet treat is also a great way to cool off in the summer. Makes three to five servings.

MATERIALS

- Large bowl
- 6 apricots (*Prunus armeniaca*) (for desire, love, romance)
- 6 cherries (*Prunus avium*) (for desire, love, lust, romance)
- 6 grapes (*Vitis vinifera*) (for desire, joy, love, passion)
- 3 kiwis (*Actinidia deliciosa*) (for happiness, joy, love, sex)
- 2 peaches (*Prunus persica*) (for desire, happiness, joy, love, sexuality)
- 2 pears (*Pyrus communis*) (for desire, love, lust)
- 1 passion fruit (*Passiflora edulis*) (for desire, love, lust, passion, sex)
- Knife
- Cutting board
- ¼ cup (60 ml) Sweet Love and Joy Powder
- 1–2 cups (250–500 ml) whipped cream
- Mixing spoon
- Plastic wrap or foil

WORKING

1. Place the bowl in the center of your work area.
2. Wash the fruit. While you wash the fruit, think about the different types of love in your life. Direct the energy and images raised into the fruit.
3. Use the knife to cut the fruit into smaller serving pieces and place them in the bowl.

4. Sprinkle the powder over the cut-up fruit.
5. Add the whipped cream to the bowl.
6. Use the spoon to combine the fruit, whipped cream, and powder. As you stir, recite 1 Corinthians 13:4–7 five times:

    Love is patient, love is kind. It does not envy, it does not boast, it is not proud. It does not dishonor others, it is not self-seeking, it is not easily angered, it keeps no record of wrongs. Love does not delight in evil but rejoices with the truth. It always protects, always trusts, always hopes, always perseveres.[9]

7. Cover the bowl with plastic wrap or foil. Chill in the fridge for eight to twelve hours before serving.

Lust, Sexuality & Fertility Spice Blends

Using magic to enhance lust and desire is just one way we can cultivate the life we want and enjoy it. The following powders are designed to boost sexuality, enhance lust, and increase fertility.

Fruit & Nut Fertility Powder

Seeds are future plants, and fruits bear the seeds of the plants they come from. When we enjoy eating

9. 1 Corinthians 13:4–7.

these foods, we can also enjoy an increase in all aspects of fertility. Remember that all the ingredients should be ground and then combined to form the final powder.

MATERIALS

- ½ cup (125 ml) cashews (*Anacardium occidentale*) (for fertility, money, success, wealth)
- ¼ cup (60 ml) peanuts (*Arachis hypogaea*) (for fertility, money, success, wealth)
- ¼ cup (60 ml) banana chips (*Musa acuminata*) (for fertility, sexuality)
- 2 tablespoons (30 ml) pine nuts (*Pinus quadrifolia*) (for fertility)
- 1 tablespoon (15 ml) poppy seeds (*Papaver somniferum*) (for fertility, love)
- 1 tablespoon (15 ml) sesame seeds (*Sesamum indicum*) (for success, prosperity)

Fertility for Me Snack Spell

Fertility comes in many forms. Success and prosperity make up one form. Having a safe and healthy pregnancy is another. This spell works to encourage both types of fertility in your life. For best results, enjoy this treat in both the morning and the evening and ensure that you are doing all mundane things necessary to increase chances of conception.

MATERIALS

- Plain yogurt (If you don't eat yogurt, you can use oatmeal, cottage cheese, or a similar food of your choosing.)
- Spoon
- Bowl
- Fruit and Nut Fertility Blend

WORKING

1. Scoop out a serving of yogurt into the bowl.
2. Add the powder to the yogurt.
3. Use the spoon to stir the mixture into the yogurt in a desoil, or clockwise, fashion. As you stir, repeat the following statement three to five times:

   Success comes to me, ensuring all my fertility.

4. Eat your snack. As the food enters your body and you go about your day, the fertile energy will be sent out into the universe, attracting fertility to you in every way.

Spice Up Sexuality Powder

Sometimes the romance and passion in long-term relationships can feel stale. Use this powder to boost passion, desire, and sexuality in you and your partner.

MATERIALS

- ½ cup (125 ml) cayenne pepper (*Capsicum annuum*) (for desire, lust, passion, sexuality)
- 1 tablespoon (15 ml) garlic powder (*Allium sativum*) (for desire, love, lust, passion, sexuality)
- 1 tablespoon (15 ml) onion powder (*Allium cepa*) (for desire, love, lust)
- ½ tablespoon (7 ml) parsley (*Petroselinum crispum*) (for desire, love, lust)
- ½ tablespoon (7 ml) rosemary (*Salvia rosmarinus*) (for desire, lust, sexuality)

Ignite Passion Dinner Spell

Serve this dinner to your partner when you want to spice up your relationship and increase the passion between the two of you. Side suggestions for this dish are mashed potatoes and corn or carrots with a maple glaze.

MATERIALS

- Ham steak
- Spice Up Sexuality Powder
- Pan
- Spatula
- Knife

WORKING

1. Rub both sides of the ham steak with the Spice Up Sexuality Powder. Make sure each side is evenly coated with the spice rub.

2. Cook the ham steak for five minutes over medium heat, then flip the steak to cook f or five more minutes.
3. Cut the ham steak and serve with any desired sides.

Sweet Heat Passion Powder

Desire and passion are hot, spicy, and sweet emotions. Use the following powder to bring sensual energy into your life.

MATERIALS

- ¾ cup (180 ml) cocoa powder (*Theobroma cacao*) (for desire, joy, passion, sensuality)
- 1½ tablespoons (22 ml) cinnamon (*Cinnamomum verum*) (for desire, love, lust, sexuality)
- 1 tablespoon (15 ml) clove (*Syzygium aromaticum*) (for desire, love)
- 1 tablespoon (15 ml) ginger (*Zingiber officinale*) (for desire, love, lust, passion, sexuality)
- ½ tablespoon (7 ml) cayenne pepper (*Capsicum annuum*) (for desire, passion, sexuality)

Luck Spice Blends

Good luck is one of the best things in the world. By eating foods that contain the following powders, you can attract luck to your life and the lives of those you care about.

Lucky Refresher Powder

This herbal powder will leave you feeling refreshed and renewed while also bringing good luck into your life.

MATERIALS

- 1 cup (250 ml) alfalfa (*Medicago sativa*) (for good luck, prosperity, success)
- 2 tablespoons (30 ml) ginger (*Zingiber officinale*) (for good luck, success, to attract luck)
- 1 tablespoon (15 ml) spearmint (*Mentha spicata*) (for prosperity, success, to attract luck)
- ½ tablespoon (7 ml) grains of paradise (*Aframomum melegueta*) (for luck, to attract good luck, protect luck)
- ½ tablespoon (7 ml) mace (*Myristica fragrans*) (for good luck, success)

Sweet, Fruity Luck Powder

Good luck is sweet, much like the fruits and spices that make up this powder. This blend pairs well with dessert foods or breakfast.

MATERIALS

- 1 cup (250 ml) sugar (*Saccharum officinarum*) (for luck, prosperity, success)
- 1½ tablespoons (22 ml) allspice (*Pimenta dioica*) (for sweetness, to attract luck)
- 1 tablespoon (15 ml) freeze-dried blueberries (*Vaccinium corymbosum*) (for good luck, sweetness, to attract luck)

- 1 tablespoon (15 ml) freeze-dried strawberry (*Fragaria ananassa*) (for luck, sweetness, to attract luck)
- ½ tablespoon (7 ml) nutmeg (*Myristica fragrans*) (for good luck, to attract luck, protect luck)
- Zest from 1 orange (*Citrus sinensis*) (for good luck, to attract luck)

Banana & Peanut Butter Luck Snack Spell

This simple snack is based on one of my favorite after-school snacks: a banana in a cup that had peanut butter and chocolate syrup drizzled over it. Today I eat the same snack but with my Sweet, Fruity Luck Powder for a burst of luck and success.

MATERIALS

- Small mug
- ¼ cup (60 ml) peanut butter (for luck, prosperity, success)
- 2 tablespoons (30 ml) Sweet, Fruity Luck Powder
- Spoon
- Small bowl
- Banana (*Musa acuminata*) (for fertility, luck, success)
- Butter knife
- Chocolate syrup
- Fork

WORKING

1. In the mug, combine the peanut butter and the magical powder.

2. When the peanut butter and powder have been thoroughly combined, place the mug in the microwave and heat for thirty-five seconds on medium-high heat.
3. Peel and slice the banana. Arrange the slices in the small bowl.
4. Drizzle the chocolate syrup over the banana slices.
5. Carefully drizzle the warmed peanut butter over the slices.
6. Enjoy the treat, adding more chocolate and peanut butter according to taste.

Fresh Good Luck Powder

Use this powder when you feel you've had some bad luck and need a batch of fresh good luck.

MATERIALS

- 1 cup (250 ml) sugar (*Saccharum officinarum*) (for attraction, good luck, success)
- 2 tablespoons (30 ml) allspice (*Pimenta dioica*) (for good luck, to attract luck)
- 1 tablespoon (15 ml) cinnamon (*Cinnamomum verum*) (for attraction, success, sweetness)
- 1 tablespoon (15 ml) nutmeg (*Myristica fragrans*) (for good luck)
- zest from 1 orange (*Citrus sinensis*) (for good luck, success, to attract luck)

Baneful Magical Powders

The following magical powders are useful in baneful workings. These powders are not to be taken or used lightly. As with all baneful magic, these powders should be used as a last resort and only with careful consideration for all lives involved.

Some of the powders included here have been presented for educational purposes only. I strongly believe that it is important to know about these practices so that, should they be used against you, you know what they are, and you can work to defend against them.

Since many of these baneful magic powders contain materials that have high levels of capsicum, you may want to wear gloves when working with and making these powders. Likewise, you may want to wear safety glasses to protect your eyes from the dust. The spices here are not ones you want to get into your eyes or even near your face.

Bad Luck Powders

Bad luck is one symptom of being cursed. Bad luck curses are simple and effective ways to create small problems in an individual's life. Use these powders when you want to slightly jinx your target and don't want anything too serious to happen.

Unlucky Day Powder

Use this powder to make someone have a day of small unlucky situations. Remember that any herb used to bring luck can also be used to remove luck.

MATERIALS

- ¾ cup (180 ml) stinging nettle leaves (*Urtica dioica*) (for bad luck)
- 2 tablespoons (30 ml) black peppercorns (*Piper nigrum*) (for bad luck, removal)
- 1 tablespoon (15 ml) allspice (*Pimenta dioica*) (for bad luck)
- 1 tablespoon (15 ml) poppy seeds (*Papaver somniferum*) (for bad luck)

Repel Good Luck Powder

Use this powder to keep good luck away from your target.

MATERIALS

- 1 cup (250 ml) magnetic sand (to repel good luck)
- 2 tablespoons (30 ml) blackberry leaves (*Rubus*) (for reversal)
- 1 tablespoon (15 ml) peony flowers (*Paeonia officinalis*) (for bad luck)
- ½ tablespoon (7 ml) mandrake root (*Mandragora officinarum*) (for bad luck, inability to sleep, nightmares)
- ½ tablespoon (7 ml) valerian root (*Valeriana officinalis*) (for baneful magic)

Luck Be Gone Spell

This spell uses Repel Good Luck Powder to keep good luck from your target.

MATERIALS

- Photo of your target or slip of paper
- Pen
- Mirror
- Small horseshoe
- Chime candleholder
- Black chime candle
- Repel Good Luck Powder
- Lighter or matches

WORKING

1. On the back of the photo or piece of paper, write your target's name and date of birth. If that information is unknown, write another way to identify your target.

2. Set the photo or paper with your target's identifying information on the mirror, with the words facing the mirror and the photo facing you.
3. Place the horseshoe upside down, making an n (symbolic of having luck spill out) over the photo or paper.
4. Place the chime candle in the holder and set it on the center of the photo or piece of paper.
5. Cover the photo or piece of paper with Repel Good Luck Powder. As you do so, think about good luck being repelled from them and bad luck sticking to them, chanting:

   From (target's name) repel good luck away.
   Bad luck alone is welcome to stay.

6. Once the photo is covered, sprinkle a layer of powder over the horseshoe, stating:

   Horseshoe of luck, bring (target's name) bad luck. Let chaos run wild, free, and amok.

7. Light the candle. As you do so, state:

   As this candle does burn, bad luck do you earn.

8. Let the candle burn completely.
9. When the candle has burned down, dispose of the photo or paper, candle remains, and powder in the trash. Find a way to give the horseshoe to

your target. As long as they have the horseshoe, bad luck will go their way.

Bad Luck Powder

This powder uses the power of several baneful herbs to surround your target with bad luck, causing them to have a lot of small misfortunes.

MATERIALS
- ¼ cup (60 ml) asafetida (*Ferula assa-foetida*) (for bad luck, ill will)
- ½ tablespoon (7ml) black mustard seed (*Brassica nigra*) (for bad luck, baneful magic)
- ½ tablespoon (7 ml) galangal root (*Alpinia galanga*) (for baneful energy)
- ½ tablespoon (7 ml) ivy (*Hedera helix*) (to entangle good luck and energy sent their way)
- ½ tablespoon (7 ml) stinging nettle leaves (*Urtica dioica*) (for baneful magic, justice)

Chaos & Confusion Powders

One of the ways that I like to hex people is through simply adding chaos and confusion to their lives. Chaos and confusion create stress. Stress then creates conflicts and other problems in life. Use these powders to bring chaos and confusion into your target's life.

Seeds of Confusion Powder

This powder uses the power of seeds to sow confusion and discord in your target's life. All of the seeds included in this powder are often used in witches' jars and balls to confuse evil spirits and baneful energy while trapped inside them.

Materials

- ¼ cup (60 ml) black mustard seed (*Brassica nigra*) (for chaos, confusion)
- ¼ cup (60 ml) poppy seeds (*Papaver somniferum*) (for chaos, confusion)
- ½ tablespoon (7 ml) dill seeds (*Anethum graveolens*) (to sour the situation)
- ½ tablespoon (7 ml) grains of paradise (*Aframomum melegueta*) (for confusion)

Decay & Chaos Powder

This powder calls upon the powers of death and decay to bring confusion into your target's life. Any order and control that they had will appear to be gone.

Materials

- ½ cup (125 ml) crushed red fire ants (for baneful magic, chaos, confusion)
- ½ tablespoon (7 ml) crushed termites or termite leavings (for baneful magic, chaos, confusion)
- ½ tablespoon (7 ml) poppy seeds (*Papaver somniferum*) (for chaos, confusion)

- ½ tablespoon (7 ml) swamp dirt (asafetida [*Ferula assa-foetida*] can be used as a substitute) (for confusion, fear)
- ½ tablespoon (7 ml) tidal dirt (gathered at low to high and high to low) (for change, chaos, confusion)

Fiery Chaos & Confusion Powder

This powder uses the destructive, fiery traits of the materials to bring discord and disharmony through confusion.

MATERIALS

- ½ cup (125 ml) cayenne pepper (*Capsicum annuum*) (for baneful magic, heat, hexing, jinxing)
- ½ tablespoon (7 ml) black mustard seed (*Brassica nigra*) (for chaos, confusion)
- ½ tablespoon (7 ml) black peppercorns (*Piper nigrum*) (for baneful magic, removal)
- ½ tablespoon (7 ml) poppy seeds (*Papaver somniferum*) (for chaos, confusion)
- ½ tablespoon (7 ml) termite leavings (for chaos, confusion)

To Create Financial Discord & Confusion Spell

This spell uses Fiery Chaos and Confusion Powder to cause just enough confusion for accounting mistakes to occur. Alternative steps are provided for those who do not cross paths with their target regularly.

MATERIALS

- Mortar and pestle
- 5 red fire ants (for chaos, confusion, luck, money, self-reliance)
- ½ tablespoon (7 ml) Fiery Chaos and Confusion Powder
- ½ tablespoon (7 ml) yellow mustard seed or ground yellow mustard seed (*Brassica alba*) (for money, prosperity)
- Small container
- Pen and paper, optional

WORKING

1. In the mortar, combine all of the materials.
2. Use the pestle to stir, crush, and combine all of the materials. As you mix the materials, think about your goal. Direct that intent into the mixture.
3. Once all of the materials have been thoroughly combined, transfer the mixture into the small container.
4. The next time you and your target are going to cross paths, sprinkle a little of the mixture directly along the route. As you scatter the mixture, state:

    Confusion and chaos come to thee. A minor hex to you from me.

As they walk over the mixture, they will bring the hex upon them.

5. If you don't cross paths with your target regularly, write their name and date of birth on the paper. If that information is unknown, write another way to identify your target.
6. Sprinkle the mixture over the paper with your target's identifying information. As you scatter the mixture, recite the following statement until the words have been covered:

    Confusion and chaos come to thee. A minor hex to you from me.

7. Once the name has been covered, crumple up the paper and powder into a small ball.
8. Toss the ball into the next trash can you find outside of your home, and let the spell do its work. After a short period of time, your spell will stop working and the chaos will calm down.

Freezing & Stopping Powders

Sometimes the best way to curse someone is to cause them to have to stop their actions. The following powders stop, freeze, or trap your target. Use these powders to teach individuals that their actions have consequences. Only once the target has learned to think before they take serious action will these curses be lifted.

Stop & Slow Down Powder

Sometimes people act and react before thinking their actions through. Use this powder when you need to get someone to stop and think before they act.

MATERIALS

- 1 tablespoon (15 ml) peppermint (*Mentha piperita*) or spearmint (*Mentha spicata*) (to cool down, freeze)
- ½ tablespoon (7 ml) belladonna (*Atropa belladonna*) (to cool down, freeze, pause/paralyze)
- ½ tablespoon (7 ml) valerian root (*Valeriana officinalis*) (to slow down, stop behaviors, for baneful magic)
- 1 teaspoon (5 ml) stop sign dirt (to stop actions)
- 10 crushed snail shells (to slow down)

To Make Someone Slow Down & Think Spell

This spell can be used to cool down a person's reaction. This is not a hex. It is a warning to wake them up before they get into trouble or hurt themselves or someone else.

MATERIALS

- Pen
- Slip of paper
- Small bowl
- Stop and Slow Down Powder
- 1 teaspoon (5 ml) molasses (to slow down, stop, for being stuck)

WORKING

1. On the paper, write your target's name and date of birth. If that information is unknown, write out another way to identify them. Then write "Slow Down and Think."
2. Set the piece of paper in the center of the bowl.
3. Sprinkle the Stop and Slow Down Powder over your target's identifying information. As you sprinkle the powder, repeat the following statement five times:

   Slow down and think it through. There is no alarm. Moving too quickly causes more harm.

4. Pour the molasses over the paper. As you do so, state:

   To sweeten and slow, to take the time to grow.

5. Place the bowl in a dark place away from direct heat, light, and moisture. Keep the paper in that dark, cool place until your target learns the desired lesson. Once they have, dispose of the materials in the trash.

Trapping Powder

Sometimes people lie, and when they do, the lies can get out of control. This powder forces individuals to face the web of lies they have made. Only once they start telling the truth will they be released from the trap of lies they wove.

MATERIALS

- ¾ cup (180 ml) kudzu (*Pueraria montana*) (to entangle lies and evil, trap evil, trip up evil)
- 2 tablespoons (30 ml) devil's shoestring (*Viburnum alnifolium*) (to entangle lies, trap evil)
- 1 tablespoon (15 ml) ivy (*Hedera helix*) (to entangle lies and evil, trap evil, trip up evil)
- 1 teaspoon (5 ml) swamp dirt (for entrapment, to get lost, get stuck)
- 3 snail shells (to slow down, stop)

Freeze & Sting Powder

Freezing those who cause problems is one way that justice can be served. The following powder allows you to freeze your target without having to perform a freezer spell.

MATERIALS

- 2½ tablespoons (37 ml) wintergreen (*Gaultheria procumbens*) (to cool down, freeze, stop)
- 2 tablespoons (30 ml) peppermint (*Mentha piperita*) (to cool down, freeze, stop)
- 1½ tablespoon (22 ml) stinging nettle (*Urtica dioica*) (for baneful magic, justice)
- 1 teaspoon (5 ml) stop sign dirt (to stop behavior)
- 10 snail shells (to confuse, freeze, slow down, stop)

General Crossing Powders

Crossing someone is another term for casting a hex or curse. The following magical powders can be used by themselves, or they can be incorporated into baneful workings to add their power.

Nightmare Fuel Powder

Use this powder to transform your target's peaceful dreams into something disturbing or terrifying, preventing them from taking any further actions against you or your loved ones.

MATERIALS

- ½ cup (125 ml) mayapple root (*Podophyllum peltatum*) (for dreams, horror, nightmares)
- ¼ cup (60 ml) mandrake root (*Mandragora officinarum*) (for dreams, horror, nightmares)
- 1½ tablespoons (22 ml) black mustard seeds (*Brassica nigra*) (for baneful magic, chaos, confusion, justice)
- 1 tablespoon (15 ml) valerian root (*Valeriana officinalis*) (for dreams, relaxation, sleep)
- ½ tablespoon (7 ml) belladonna (*Atropa belladonna*) (to cool off, freeze, pause/paralyze)

To Cause Nightmares Spell

Use this spell to cause your target to have a series of nightmares. Until your target learns their behaviors and attitudes are causing the nightmares, they will have a different nightmare every night.

MATERIALS

- Fashion doll with removeable head (The doll should match your target's gender.)
- Nightmare Fuel Powder
- Pin, needle, or knife
- Black pillar candle
- Small plate
- Lighter or matches
- 3 black-headed pins

WORKING

1. Remove the head from the fashion doll and fill it with Nightmare Fuel Powder. As you fill the doll's head, state:

   Nightmares for (target's name).

2. Return the head to the body of the doll. Set the doll down in the center of your work area.
3. Use the pin, needle, or knife to carve the word "Nightmare" into two or three sides of the candle.
4. Rub any remaining Nightmare Fuel Powder onto the candle from bottom to top.
5. Place the candle on the plate directly behind the fashion doll.
6. Light the candle.

7. Carefully pass each pin through the flame of the candle three times and then stab it into the head of the doll, placing one in the front, one in the center, and one in the back of the head.
8. Continue to let the candle burn for thirty minutes.
9. After thirty minutes, extinguish the candle, and set the candle and doll somewhere they will not be disturbed.
10. Once a day, until the candle has completely burned, place the candle, plate, and doll in the center of your work area and burn the candle.
11. When the candle has finished burning, dispose of the candle in the trash. Remove the pins from the doll's head and empty the powder from the head into the trash. The spell is now released.

Citrus Sour Power Powder

An easy way to jinx people is to cause their life to go sideways or "sour" for a short time. This powder is a way to sour your targets without the use of vinegar.

Materials

- ½ cup (125 ml) lemon zest (*Citrus limon*) (for baneful magic, justice, souring your target)
- ½ cup (125 ml) lime zest (*Citrus aurantifolia*) (for baneful magic, justice, souring your target)

- 2 tablespoons (30 ml) dill (*Anethum graveolens*) (for baneful magic, justice, to sour)
- 1 tablespoon (15 ml) bilberries (*Vaccinium myrtillus*) (for bitter luck)
- 1 tablespoon (15 ml) blueberries (*Vaccinium corymbosum*) (to bring sadness and sorrow)

Liar, Lips on Fire Powder

Spreading false gossip or lies is a terrible thing to do. This powder is designed to cause those who spread gossip and rumors to be burned by their actions.

MATERIALS

- 1¼ cup (310 ml) chia seeds (*Salvia hispanica*) (to stop gossip)
- 2 tablespoons (30 ml) cayenne pepper (*Capsicum annuum*) (for justice, to stop gossip)
- 1½ tablespoons (22 ml) lemon zest (*Citrus limon*) (to sour, for baneful magic, justice)
- 1 tablespoon (15 ml) jalapeño pepper (*Capsicum annuum 'Jalapeño'*) (for baneful magic, fire, justice, spice, to stop gossip)
- ½ tablespoon (7 ml) galangal root (*Alpinia galanga*) (for baneful magic, fire, justice, spice)
- ½ tablespoon (7 ml) ginger (*Zingiber officinale*) (for baneful magic, fire, justice, spice)

Stop Gossip Candle Spell

Use this spell to cause an individual who is gossiping to have pain in their mouth every time they spread false truths or misinformation.

MATERIALS

- Lip-shaped candle
- Knife
- Pen
- Slip of paper
- Liar, Lips on Fire Powder
- Black thread
- Needle
- Lighter or matches

WORKING

1. Cut an opening across the center of the wax lips.
2. Use the knife to mark a series of Xs across the lips.
3. On the paper, write out the name of the person who is gossiping about you or your loved one.
4. Stuff the slip of paper into the opening of the wax lips.
5. Cover the slip of paper with Liar, Lips on Fire Powder.
6. Thread the needle, and sew along the X lines. It does not need to look pretty. It just needs to look like lips have been sewn shut.

7. Light the candle. As you do so, state:

    Until not to gossip you do learn, with each gossip your lips shall burn.

8. Let the candle burn. If you are unable to burn the entire candle in one sitting, burn the candle for fifteen minutes a day until the candle has completely burned.
9. Once the candle has burned down, toss all remains in the trash.

Reflection & Reversal Powders

Reflection magic is sometimes considered gray magic. While the caster of a reflection or reversal spell did not cast the original hex, the hex is still being sent and directed at someone. This means that by proxy, when the hex hits its caster, you were the one who made that happen.

I look at using reflection or reversal magic as no different than if I were to use a penknife or keys between my fingers in response to being attacked by someone else. With both reversal spells and the penknife or keys, I am simply defending myself against harm.

Reversal Powder #1

This is a very simple powder that removes baneful magic from you and sends it back to the person who sent it.

MATERIALS

- 1¼ cup (310 ml) stinging nettle leaves (*Urtica dioica*) (for reflection, removal of curses and hexes, reversal)
- 2 tablespoons (30 ml) asafetida (*Ferula assa-foetida*) (for reflection, reversal)
- 1½ tablespoon (22 ml) agrimony (*Agrimonia eupatoria*) (for reflection, reversal)
- 1 tablespoon (15 ml) lemon zest (*Citrus limon*) (for reflection, to return to sender)
- ½ tablespoon (7 ml) angelica root (*Angelica archangelica*) (for removal of hexes or baneful magic)

Reversal Powder #2

Use this powder as an alternative to the first reversal powder. Any baneful magic that is not reversed is neutralized and returned to the earth.

MATERIALS

- 1 cup (250 ml) sulfur (for jinxing, justice, reversal)
- 1½ tablespoon (22 ml) blackberry leaves (*Rubus*) (for reflection, reversal)
- 1 tablespoon (15 ml) black peppercorns (*Piper nigrum*) (to return to sender)
- 1 tablespoon (15 ml) stinging nettle leaves (*Urtica dioica*) (for reflection, reversal, to return to sender)
- ½ tablespoon (7 ml) cayenne pepper (*Capsicum annuum*) (for fire, justice, speed, to return to sender)

Return with Justice Powder

This magical powder reverses any hex sent your way, returning the spell to its sender. As an added bonus, justice for the actions taken returns with the hex to keep the attacker from hurting or messing with you or your loved ones again.

MATERIALS

- 1 cup (250 ml) blackberry leaves (*Rubus*) (for reflection, reversal, to return to sender)
- 1½ tablespoons (22 ml) galangal root (*Alpinia galanga*) (for justice, protection, reflection, reversal, to return to sender)
- 1 tablespoon (15 ml) rue (*Ruta graveolens*) (for reflection, reversal, to return to sender)
- 1 tablespoon (15 ml) stinging nettle leaves (*Urtica dioica*) (for hex breaking, reversal, to return to sender)
- ½ tablespoon (7 ml) asafetida (*Ferula assa-foetida*) (for baneful magic, justice, hex breaking)

Return to Sender Justice Jar Spell

This working is a justice spell and a reversal spell. Use it when you have been attacked mundanely or magically without reason. It works best when you need to return justice to someone wrongly accusing or harming you.

MATERIALS

- Small mason jar with lid
- Mirror fragments or broken glass
- Return with Justice Powder
- 5 needles
- 1 tablespoon devil's shoestring (*Viburnum alnifolium*) (for justice, to reflect baneful magic)
- 5 blackthorn thorns (*Prunus spinosa*) (for baneful magic, justice)
- 1 tablespoon (15 ml) rue (*Ruta graveolens*) (for baneful magic, justice)

WORKING

1. Add the mirror fragments or broken glass to the jar. State:

   To reflect back that which I consider an attack.

2. Pour half of the Return with Justice Powder into the jar. As you pour the powder, repeat the following statement three times:

   Justice I seek today, return ill will for the crime they shall pay.

3. Add the needles to the jar. State:

   Needles to attack and return justice back.

4. Add the devil's shoestring to the jar. State:

   To entangle and trap ill will to send back.

5. Add the thorns. State:

   Thorns to prick and defend those I call family or friend.

6. Add the rue. As you add the herb, spit and state:

    A curse to (name 0-----of individual who has targeted you) that you cannot reverse.

7. Seal the jar and shake it to mix the materials. As you shake the jar, repeat the statement from step 2 five times.
8. Once a day, repeat step 7 until you feel the target has learned their lesson.
9. To release the spell, unseal the lid of the jar and dispose of the contents in the trash. You can cleanse the jar and use it in future magical works.

Hot Foot Powders

Hot foot powder is a classic type of baneful powder. If you were to ask someone how to quickly remove someone from their life, the response would almost always be hot footing. Whether it's a troublesome neighbor or a coworker who needs to be removed, hot foot powder is the answer. There are many ways to hot foot an individual, and I share my three favorite powder formulas here.

As with all baneful workings, it is important to ensure that only the target of the spell will be hit with the magic. One thing to be careful about is that with hot foot powders, your target can end up with stability issues. If you are not specific about your intent to have them move away, they might have issues with employment, such as their job moving, or relationship problems, such as being forced to leave their family. These issues will then ripple outward, affecting other people.

Hot Foot Powder #1

This powder is one of the more traditional forms of hot foot powder, as it uses crushed red fire ants as well as botanical materials. When crafting and using this powder, wear gloves to protect yourself from the sting that fire ants have even when dead.

MATERIALS

- 10 red fire ants (for baneful magic, heat, to move away, sting)
- ½ dirt dauber's nest (for chaos of moving, removal, to attack, sting)
- 2 tablespoons (30 ml) cayenne pepper (*Capsicum annuum*) (for heat, removal, to move away)
- 1 tablespoon (15 ml) black peppercorns (*Piper nigrum*) (for baneful magic, removal, to move away)
- 1 teaspoon (5 ml) dirt from a transportation center (for moving away)

Hot Foot Powder #2

This is an herbal-only variation of hot foot powder. Use this powder when you want to hot foot someone but aren't willing to work with fire ants. Due to the spices involved with crafting hot foot powder, you may want to use gloves in the creation of this formula as well.

MATERIALS

- ¾ cup (180 ml) cayenne pepper (*Capsicum annuum*) (for baneful magic, heat, removal, to move away)
- 1 tablespoon (15 ml) black peppercorns (*Piper nigrum*) (for baneful magic, heat, removal, speed)
- 1 tablespoon (15 ml) galangal root (*Alpinia galanga*) (for baneful magic, removal)
- ½ tablespoon (7 ml) poppy seeds (*Papaver somniferum*) (for chaos, confusion from moving)
- ½ tablespoon (7 ml) stinging nettle leaves (*Urtica dioica*) (for baneful magic, removal, to return to sender)

Hot Foot Chaos Spell

For this spell, you need to know the name of your target. If you do not know their name, you need to have some way to identify them so that only your target will be hit by the spell.

Use this spell when you want to hot foot someone and want that move to be extra chaotic. The chaos and stress of moving is difficult for everyone, and this spell magnifies that hectic energy for your target.

MATERIALS

- Pin, needle, or knife
- Black chime candle
- Chime candleholder
- Mortar and pestle
- Fiery Chaos and Confusion Powder

- Hot Foot Powder #2
- Pen
- Paper
- Lighter or matches

WORKING

1. Use the pin, needle, or knife to carve the words "Chaos and Removal" into the chime candle. Set the candle in the holder.
2. In the mortar, combine the two powders. While mixing the baneful powders together, repeat the following statement seven times:

   A curse for (target's name) today. Chaos and confusion sent your way.

3. On the paper, write out your target's name and date of birth. If that information is unknown, write out another way to identify your target.
4. Set the paper under the candleholder.
5. Sprinkle the powder mixture around the candle and over the paper. You want to use all of the powder and cover the paper as much as possible.
6. Light the candle and let it burn completely.
7. Once the candle has finished burning and the wax is cool to the touch, gather the candle wax, paper, and powder together.
8. Take the gathered materials to a trash can outside of and away from your home. Toss the materials

into the trash. As you do so, spit into the trash can, repeating the statement from step 2.

9. Walk away and return home. When you get home, cleanse yourself through your preferred cleansing rituals. I prefer showers or an egg cleanse. To do the latter, take an egg and rub it down your body, starting at your crown and ending at your feet. Then crack the egg into either a large glass of water or the toilet and flush it down the toilet.

Hot Foot Powder #3

This is the most potent form of hot foot powder I know. Use this powder when you truly need to get someone gone and out of your life.

MATERIALS

- 1 cup (250 ml) sulfur (for baneful magic, heat, power)
- ¼ cup (60 ml) any hot pepper (for baneful magic, heat, to move away, sting)
- ½ tablespoon (7 ml) dirt from an ant mound (for baneful magic, heat, to move away, sting)
- ½ tablespoon (7 ml) termite leavings (for baneful magic, chaos, confusion, heat, to move away, sting)
- 1 teaspoon (5 ml) graveyard dirt (for baneful magic)
- 5 red fire ants (for baneful magic, heat, to move away, sting)

Goofer Dust

Finally, I want to share a traditional cursing powder used in Conjure work: Goofer Dust. This dust has a long history in baneful magic and is a nasty material to create. Author Judika Illes provides an excellent history on Goofer Dust in her *Encyclopedia of 5,000 Spells*. She writes, "'*Goofer*' derives from the Kinkongo word '*kufwa*,' meaning 'to die,' and 99.5 percent of Goofer Dust's uses are malevolent."[10] She continues, writing that "Goofer Dust allegedly causes the target of the spell to become weak and confused. Powers of speech, concentration, and thought are allegedly affected; the target acts '*goofy*.'"[11]

Goofer Dust is one of the most potent forms of baneful magic out there. Due to the power behind them, Goofer Dust powders should only be used in extreme circumstances. If there are other baneful methods that can be used to address your problem, try them before turning to Goofer Dust. Goofer Dust is a last-resort hex.

Goofer Dust #1

There are many formulas for Goofer Dust out there. This version is likely the easiest one to create, as the materials are fairly easy to obtain.

10. Illes, *The Encyclopedia of 5,000 Spells*, 1,058.
11. Illes, *The Encyclopedia of 5,000 Spells*, 1,058.

MATERIALS

- ½ cup (125 ml) gunpowder (for baneful magic, death, destruction)
- 2 tablespoons (30 ml) used cat litter (for baneful magic, hexing)
- 1 tablespoon (15 ml) valerian root (*Valeriana officinalis*) (for fear, nightmares)
- ½ tablespoon (7 ml) poppy seeds (*Papaver somniferum*) (for confusion)
- 1 teaspoon (5 ml) graveyard dirt (for death)

Goofer Dust #2

This is a secondary formula for Goofer Dust. Both this formula and the third formula are shared for informative purposes. I sincerely hope that using Goofer Dust is not something you ever have to do.

MATERIALS

- ½ cup (60 ml) sulfur (for baneful magic, confusion, death, decay)
- 1 tablespoon (15 ml) black mustard seed (*Brassica nigra*) (for chaos, confusion)
- ½ tablespoon (7 ml) asafetida (*Ferula assa-foetida*) (for confusion, decay, fear, rot)
- ½ tablespoon (7 ml) stinging nettle leaves (*Urtica dioica*) (for baneful magic, to sting)

Destroy My Enemy Curse

This spell is for when you just need your enemy to be gone and out of your life. This is a last resort spell. Try other methods of dealing with your enemy before turning to this working.

MATERIALS

- Pen
- Paper
- Small bowl
- Modeling clay
- Goofer Dust #2
- Decay and Chaos Powder
- Dirt dauber nest (for attacks, baneful magic, chaos, confusion, destruction of your enemy)
- 9 pins or needles

WORKING

1. On the paper, write the name of your enemy. If you know their date of birth, include that information as well.
2. In the small bowl, place the clay, Goofer Dust, and the Decay and Chaos Powder. Use your hands to knead the clay, thoroughly mixing the powders into the clay.
3. Break the clay into six small pieces. Each of those balls will be used to build the clay dolly for this spell.
4. Work a piece of clay around the paper with your target's name. Make sure the words are competently covered by the clay.

5. Place a second ball of clay on top of the clay you just wrapped around the paper. This ball will become the head of the doll.
6. Work two balls of clay into arms. Once you have those set, attach them to the body.
7. Finish the clay dolly with the last two pieces of clay, forming them into legs. When you feel comfortable with how they look, attach them to the body.
8. Hold the finished clay figure in your hands. Exhale over the figure and state:

    Clay doll, I name you (your target's name).

9. Cover the doll with the dirt dauber nest. As you do so, visualize wasps attacking your victim.
10. Once the doll has been covered, stab the pins or needles into the dolly one at a time. As you stab the doll, direct all of your anger and frustrations out on the figure. With each stab, state:

    For the evil you sent my way, it is now time to pay.

11. Starting with the head, stab five pins or needles down the center. Use the remaining four to pin the arms and legs.
12. Set the clay dolly somewhere in the dark where it will not be disturbed. Leave the dolly alone until you feel that your target has learned their lesson and is no longer causing problems.

13. When it is time to release the spell, take out each of the pins and set them aside to be washed in hot, soapy water. Dig the paper out of the center of the body. Toss the clay into the trash. If it is possible to burn the paper, do so. Otherwise, toss the paper into the trash with the clay. This releases the spell.

Goofer Dust #3

This is the final variation of Goofer Dust I will share with you. There are hundreds of different formulas, each one creating a different type of curse from the materials.

MATERIALS

- 1 cup (250 ml) mandrake root (*Mandragora officinarum*) (for nightmares)
- ¼ cup (60 ml) dried animal dung (for baneful magic, to make things go to crud)
- 1 tablespoon (15 ml) blackthorn bark (*Prunus spinosa*) (for baneful magic, nightmares)
- 1 tablespoon (15 ml) graveyard dirt (for ancestors, baneful magic)
- 1 tablespoon (15 ml) gunpowder (for baneful magic, death, destruction)
- 1 tablespoon (15 ml) poppy seeds (*Papaver somniferum*) (for chaos, confusion)
- 1 tablespoon (15 ml) sulfur (for baneful magic, confusion, death, decay)

PART III
Resources

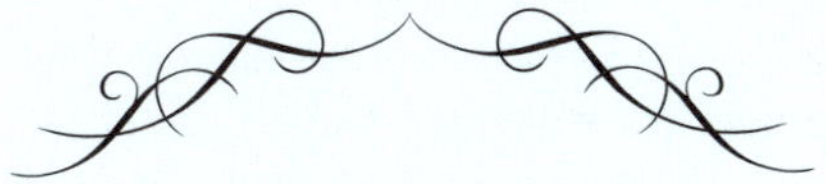

Animal Correspondences

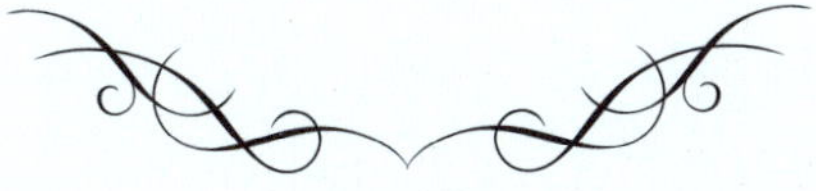

Working with the power of animals provides a unique perspective of the world, magic, and how everything is connected. Using animal curios found in nature or from the remains of an animal has long been a part of magical practices. Working with animal curios can help you develop a spiritual and magical connection with the animals of this world, and their wisdom can guide you forward.

This section contains an A–Z list of animal curios that were used throughout this book, whether in a powder formula or a working that used a powder. Look through the correspondences here, and use the meanings as a starting point for developing your own magical relationships with these spirits and forces.

Alligator Claws: Attracting luck, good luck

Ants, General: Block busting, chaos, confusion, luck, money, perseverance, self-reliance, success

Bee Pollen: Healing, health, prosperity, success, wellness

Bees: Industriousness, loyalty, perseverance, protection, sweetness

Beetles: Block busting, protection, removal of barriers

Butterfly Chrysalis: Beauty, self-love, renewal

Butterfly Wings: Beauty, self-love, renewal

Cat Claws: Defense, protection, strength

Cat's Eye Shells: Protection against the evil eye

Chicken Shells: Cascarilla powder base, cleansing, hex breaking, protection, removal

Clam Shells: Protection

Crab Claws: Cutting, removal, reversal

Dirt Dauber Nests: Attacking, chaos or moving, removal, sting

Dragonflies: Beauty, call dragons, draconic power, dragon spirits, grace

Fire Ants: Baneful magic, chaos, confusion, heat, move away, sting

Lobster Claws: Cutting, removal

Rabbit's Foot: Good luck

Sea Shell, General: Protection

Snail Shells: Protection, protection against behaviors, slowing down, stopping, stopping behavior

Snake Skin: Healing, renewal

Termite Leavings: Baneful magic, chaos, confusion

Wasps: Fertility, life, prosperity, success

Wolf Fur: Camouflage, invisibility, power, protection, strength

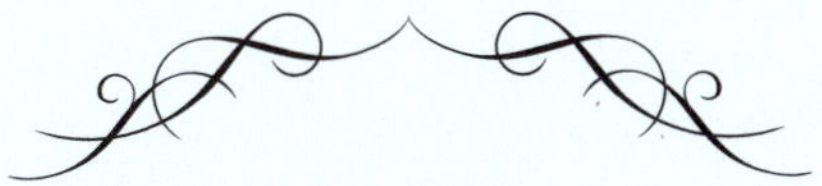

Herb Correspondences

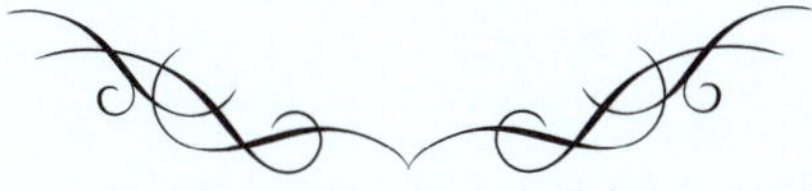

When it comes to magic, *herbs* essentially means any plant of a part that is worked with. From trees, weeds, and spices in your kitchen to flowers in your garden and roots deep in the earth, all of these materials are considered herbs in the magical world.

This is an A–Z listing of all the herbal materials used in this book. They were either an ingredient in a magical powder, or they were used in a spell to heighten the power of the magical powder.

Use this listing of correspondences to create your own magical correspondences and develop your own powders.

Abre Camino (*Koanophyllon villosum*): Block busting, cleansing, hex breaking, overcoming obstacles, road opening, victory

Acorn/Oak (*Quercus* spp.): Fertility, masculinity, power, strength, symbol of the Horned God

African Violet (*Saintpaulia ionantha*): Mental focus, psychic power, psychic senses

Agrimony (*Agrimonia eupatoria*): Banishment, cleansing, exorcism, protection, removal, reversal

Alfalfa (*Medicago sativa*): Fast cash, luck, money, prosperity, success

Allheal (*Prunella vulgaris*): Healing, health, protection against illness, wellness

Allspice (*Pimenta dioica*): Attraction, friendship, good luck, healing, health, love, luck, money, prosperity, protection of luck, success, wealth, wellness

Angelica Root (*Angelica archangelica*): Angelic forces, banishment, blessings, exorcism, healing, hex breaking, neutralization of baneful energy, protection, protection against baneful magic, spiritual strength, strength

Anise Seed (*Illicium verum*): Divination, good luck, magic, psychic abilities, psychic dreams, psychic gifts, psychic senses, trance work, wish granting

Apricot (*Prunus armeniaca*): Desire, love, romance

Arnica (*Arnica montana*): Astral travel, protection, protection from spiritual forces, psychic powers

Asafetida (*Ferula assa-foetida*): Bad luck, baneful magic, chaos, confusion, fear, hex breaking, ill will, justice, protection against baneful magic, reversal

Ash (*Fraxinus excelsior*): Desire, healing, love, prophetic dreams, protection, prosperity, wealth

Banana (*Musa acuminata*): Fertility, sexuality

Basil (*Ocimum basilicum*): Ancestor work, attracting spirits, cleansing, dragon spirits, dragon work, exorcism, luck, money, prosperity, protection, removal, removal of blocks, road opening, success, underworld work

Bay Leaf (*Laurus nobilis*): Block busting, road opening, strength

Belladonna (*Atropa belladonna*): Cooling off, freezing, pausing/paralyzing

Benzoin (*Styrax paralleloneurus*): Protection against theft

Bilberry (*Vaccinium myrtillus*): Bitter luck, generating luck, generating wealth, protection

Birch (*Betula pendula*): Healing, protection, purification

Blackberry (*Rubus*): Luck, money, protection, removal, reversal, success

Black-Eyed Susan (*Rudbeckia hirta*): Ancestor work, cleansing, connecting with the dead, grounding, releasing, underworld work

Black Peppercorns (*Piper nigrum*): Baneful magic, banishment, cleansing, exorcism, heat, protection, reflect magic, removal, repel evil, return to sender, reversal, speed

Blackthorn (*Prunus spinosa*): Baneful magic, justice, protection

Blueberry (*Vaccinium corymbosum*): Money, prosperity, wealth

Cardamom (*Elettaria cardamomum*): Attract luck, desire, love, lust, passion

Carrot (*Daucus carota*): Eye health, fertility, success, underworld

Cashew (*Anacardium occidentale*): Money, prosperity, success, wealth

Catnip (*Nepeta cataria*): Anxiety relief, baneful magic, cats, feline power, friendship, happiness, health, joy, peace, psychic senses, psychic sight, viciousness, wellness

Cayenne Pepper (*Capsicum annuum*): Baneful magic, desire, heat, hexing, jinxing, justice, lust, passion, power, protection, reflection, removal, sexuality, speed

Cedar (*Cedrus libani*): Cleansing, healing, hex breaking, money, protection, purification, removal

Celery Seed (*Apium graveolens*): Concentration, lust, mental clarity, psychic abilities, psychic dreams, psychic senses

Chamomile (*Matricaria recutita*): Anxiety relief, depression relief, dreams, good luck, growth, happiness, healing, money, peace, prosperity, psychic powers, sleep, success, wealth

Chervil (*Anthriscus cerefolium*): Joy, peace, spiritual growth, wisdom

Cherry (*Prunus avium*): Desire, love, lust, romance

Chia Seeds (*Salvia hispanica*): Health, prosperity, protecting yourself, protection, stop gossip, strength

Cinnamon (*Cinnamomum verum*): Attraction, blessing, block breaking, cleansing, desire, fast cash, love, luck, lust, money, passion, prosperity, protection, removal, romance, speed, success, sweetness

Cinquefoil (*Potentilla canadensis*): Attraction, fast cash, good luck, money, prosperity, success, wealth

Clove (*Syzygium aromaticum*): Astral travel, desire, divination, love, lust, mental clarity, passion, psychic abilities, psychic travels, relationships, spiritual work, sweetness

Clover (*Trifolium repens*): Good luck, happiness, love, peace, sweetness

Cocoa Powder (*Theobroma cacao*): Anxiety relief, attraction, desire, friendship, happiness, love, lust, money, self-love, stress relief, success, sweetness, wealth

Coffee (*Coffea arabica*): Cleansing, concentration, divination, energy, focus, hex breaking, mood uplifting, power

Copal (*Bursera odorata*): Angelic blessings, cleansing, consecration, love, protection, purification, spirituality

Coriander (*Coriandrum sativum*): Desire, good luck, healing, lust

Cramp Bark (*Viburnum opulus*): Attracting luck, good luck, healing, protect luck, protection

Cumin (*Cuminum cyminum*): Deflecting baneful energy, deflecting evil, removal, reversal

Daffodil (*Narcissus*): Beauty, fertility, love, luck

Daisy (*Chrysanthemum leucanthemum*): Depression relief, friendship, happiness, innocence, joy, love, lust, mood lifting, passion

Damiana Leaf (*Turnera diffusa*): Astral travel, desire, lust, meditation, passion, psychic powers, psychic work, sexuality

Dandelion (*Taraxacum officinale*): Attraction, fast cash, financial fertility, money, prosperity, success, wealth, wishes

Devil's Shoestring (*Viburnum alnifolium*): Entangling baneful energy, good luck, justice, keeping law away, protecting your good luck, protection, reflecting baneful energy

Dill (*Anethum graveolens*): Attracting good luck, desire, fast cash, good luck, hex breaking, keeping law away, lust, passion, sexuality, souring individuals, souring the situation, success

Dragon's Blood (*Dracaena cinnabari*): Cleansing, desire, dragon energy, dragon power, fire, lust, magic, money, passion, power, prosperity, protection, removal, sexuality, success, wealth, wishes

Elderflower (*Sambucus nigra*): Cleansing, exorcism, prosperity, protection, protection against baneful magic, sleep

Eyebright (*Euphrasia rostkoviana*): Mental powers, psychic sight, spiritual sight

Fennel Seed (*Foeniculum vulgare*): Cleansing, protection, warding against evil

Fenugreek (*Trigonella foenum-graecum*): Fast cash, good luck, money, prosperity, sales, success

Frankincense (*Boswellia sacra*): Angels, attracting spirits, blessing, cleansing, consecration, making things sacred, power, protection

Fumitory (*Fumaria officinalis*): Money, success, wealth

Galangal Root (*Alpinia galanga*): Bad luck, baneful energy, fast cash, getting money owed, justice, prosperity, protection, reflecting and return baneful energy, returning to sender, reversal, success

Garlic (*Allium sativum*): Banishment, desire, love, lust, protection, protection against evil, protection against theft, relationships, removal, repelling evil, warding against the evil eye

Ginger (*Zingiber officinale*): Fire, growth, love, luck, lust, money, passion, power, prosperity, protection against evil, protection of growth, relationships, speed, spice, success

Ginkgo Leaf (*Ginkgo biloba*): Clarity of mind and thought, healing, health, meditation, mental clarity, mental focus, mental powers, psychic abilities, trance work, wellness

Ginseng (*Panax ginseng*): Attracting luck, desire, energy, fertility, fire, growth, lust, passion, success, wish granting

Goldenrod (*Solidago altissima*): Divination, money, prosperity, success

Goldenseal (*Hydrastis canadensis*): Healing, health, wellness

Grains of Paradise (*Aframomum melegueta*): Attraction, confusion, desire, good luck, love, luck, lust, passion, prosperity, removal, success, wish granting

Grape (*Vitis vinifera*): Desire, love, joy, passion

Gravel Root (*Eutrochium purpureum*): Employment, luck

Habanero Pepper (*Capsicum chinese*): Baneful magic, fire, heat, protection, speed

Hawthorn (*Crataegus*): Ability to see and travel to the lands of the fae, fairies, fertility, luck, protection, success

Hazel (*Corylus cornuta*): Divination, fertility, luck, protection, wish granting

High John the Conqueror (*Ipomoea jalapa*): Power, protection, strength

Honeysuckle (*Lonicera caprifolium*): Drawing closer together, family, home, love, peaceful home, protecting love in the home, protecting peace in the home, sweetening

Horseradish (*Cochlearia armoracia*): Banishment, cleansing, exorcism, hex breaking, purification, removal, reversal

Hyssop (*Hyssopus officinalis*): Cleansing, hex breaking, neutralization of energy, protection, purification, reversal

Ivy (*Hedera helix*): Camouflage, entangling energy, healing, hiding, protection, trapping evil

Jalapeño Pepper (*Capsicum annuum 'Jalapeño'*): Baneful magic, banishment, energy, fire, heat, justice, power, protection, reflection, removal, spice

Jasmine (*Jasminum grandiflorum*): Divination, family, friendship, love, prophetic dreams, psychic powers, relationships, romance

Juniper (*Juniperus communis*): Banishment, exorcism, hex breaking, protection, removal

Kiwifruit (*Actinidia deliciosa*): Happiness, joy, love, sex

Kudzu (*Pueraria montana*): Entangling evil, fast growth, trapping

Lavender (*Lavandula officinalis*): Anxiety relief, cleansing, cooling, depression relief, healing, meditation, peace, peace in the home, protection, psychic development, psychic powers, spiritual work, sweetening

Lemon (*Citrus limon*): Cleansing, justice (aimed toward the individual you are cutting out), love, removal, souring

Lemon Balm (*Melissa officinalis*): Attracting love, blessings, cleansing, general love, protection, relationships, removal

Lemongrass (*Cymbopogon citratus*): Cleansing, desire, lust, psychic powers, removal

Lemon Verbena (*Lippia citriodora*): Love, purification

Lilac (*Syringa vulgaris*): Banishment, protection against baneful magic, removal

Lily (*Lilium*): Keeping unwanted visitors away, love, protection, protection against the evil eye, removal of love spells

Lime (*Citrus aurantifolia*): Cleaning, cleansing, justice, removal, souring

Lovage (*Levisticum officinale*): Attention, attraction, desire, love

Mace (*Myristica fragrans*): Attracting good luck, banishment, protection, psychic powers, removal, repelling evil

Mandrake (*Mandragora officinarum*): Ancestors, bad luck, fertility, health, inability to sleep, love, money, nightmares, protection, underworld work

Marigold (*Calendula officinalis*): Healing, health, legal matters, money, prophetic dreams, prosperity, protection, psychic development, psychic powers

Marjoram (*Origanum majorana*): Attracting happiness and joy, driving off forces that would harm your family, happiness, joy, love, lust, protection, repelling unwanted attention

Masterwort (*Astrantia major*): Control, demanding attention, domination, influencing others, power, protection

Mayapple Root (*Podophyllum peltatum*): Ancestor work, bad luck, fertility, health, inability to sleep, love, money, nightmares, underworld work

Meadowsweet (*Filipendula ulmaria*): Attracting luck, happiness, joy, love, luck, peace

Mexican Marigold (*Tagetes lemmonii*): Ancestor work, employment, healing, luck, money, prosperity, protecting money, psychic development, psychic dreams, spiritual work, success, underworld work

Mugwort (*Artemisia vulgaris*): Blessing, cleansing, divination, power of magic and witchcraft, prophetic dreams, psychic abilities, psychic development, spirituality, trance work

Mullein (*Verbascum thapsus*): Divination, health, love, protection

Mustard Seed, Black (*Brassica nigra*): Bad luck, baneful magic, chaos, confusion, justice, protection

Mustard Seed, White/Yellow (*Brassica alba*): Attracting luck, faith, luck, money, prosperity, reversal, success, warding evil

Myrrh (*Commiphora myrrha*): Angel work, attracting spirits, blessing, cleansing, meditation, mental focus, power, protection, spirituality

Nutmeg (*Myristica fragrans*): Attracting luck, attraction, fidelity, good luck, love, luck when gambling, money, prosperity, relationships, sales, success

Onion (*Allium cepa*): Desire, love, lust, money, protection, relationships, removal, repelling evil, wealth

Orange (*Citrus sinensis*): Attracting luck, cleansing blocks, depression relief, good luck, happiness, love, money, mood stabilization, prosperity, removing bad luck, success

Oregano (*Origanum vulgare*): Cleansing, keeping away toxic traits, protection, removal, repelling unwanted individuals

Paprika: Desire, love, passion, success, sweetness

Parsley (*Petroselinum crispum*): Ancestor work, cleansing, the dead, protection, protection against unwanted energy, removal, repelling miasma, road opening, underworld work

Passion Fruit (*Passiflora edulis*): Desire, love, lust, passion, sex

Passionflower (*Passiflora incarnata*): Friendships, love, peace, peace in the home, relationships, romance

Patchouli (*Pogostemon cablin*): Ancestor work, desire, honoring the dead, love, lust, passion, sexuality, underworld work, working with the dead

Peach (*Actinidia deliciosa*): Desire, happiness, joy, love, sexuality

Peanut (*Arachis hypogaea*): Fertility, money, success, wealth

Pear (*Pyrus communis*): Desire, love, lust

Pennyroyal (*Mentha pulegium*): Attracting good luck, attracting people, friendship, good luck, peace, peace in the home, protection, relationships, removing bad luck, socialization, strength

Peony (*Paeonia officinalis*): Attracting luck, bad luck, banishment, blessings of luck, good luck, protection against evil

Peppermint (*Mentha piperita*): Anxiety relief, calming, cleansing, cooling, healing, love, meditation, mental clarity, mental focus, peace, psychic development, relaxation, stress relief, wellness

Pine (*Pinus* spp.): Cleansing, fertility, healing, life after death, money, prosperity, protection, removal, success, success through hard financial times, underworld work, wealth

Pineapple (*Ananas comosus*): Healing, health, wellness

Plantain (*Plantago major*): Power, protection, resilience, strength

Poppy (*Papaver somniferum*): Altered states of consciousness, bad luck, chaos, confusion, divination, fertility, good luck, love, money, psychic abilities, trance work

Raspberry (*Rubus idaeus* var. *strigosus*): Money, prosperity, wealth

Rose (*Rosa rubiginosa*):

Pink: Family love, friendship, happiness, joy, kindness, love, self-esteem

Red: Desire, love, lust, passion, protection of love, relationships, romance

Thorns: Breaking up relationships, protection of love, removal of love, separation of lovers

Rosemary (*Salvia rosmarinus*): Clarity of thought, cleansing, communication, depression relief, healing, listen to me, opening minds, peace in the home, protection of peace, removal

Rue (*Ruta graveolens*): Baneful magic, banishment, cleansing, hex breaking, protection, reversal, spell removal

Sage (*Salvia officinalis*): Blessing, cleansing, protection, protection against the evil eye, protection against unwanted spirits, removal

Saint-John's-Wort (*Hypericum perforatum*): Depression relief, divination, healing, health, protection, strength

Sesame (*Sesamum indicum*): Attracting customers, money, prosperity, success, wealth

Snow Pea (*Pisum sativum* var. *macrocarpon*): Money, prosperity, success, wealth

Spearmint (*Mentha spicata*): Cooling down, freezing, healing, love, meditation, mental clarity, mental development, mental focus, peace, psychic development, relaxation, soothing

Stinging Nettle (*Urtica dioica*): Bad luck, baneful magic, banishment, cleansing, hex breaking, justice, protection, removal, repelling attention, returning to sender, reversal

Strawberry (*Fragaria ananassa*): Attracting luck, luck, sweetness

Sugar (*Saccharum officinarum*): Attracting good luck, attraction, desire, joy, kindness, love, lust, opening others to your view, passion, prosperity, sales, speed, sticking to you, success, sweetening people, sweetness

Sunflower (*Helianthus annuus*): Happiness, hope, joy, life, money, prosperity, solar energy, success, sunshine, wealth

Sweet Bell Pepper (*Capsicum annuum*): Fertility, health, money, sweetness, wealth

Thyme (*Thymus vulgaris*): Cleansing, good luck, love, protection, purification, strength, underworld travel

Tomato (*Solanum lycopersicum*): Desire, love, passion, relationships

Turmeric (*Curcuma longa*): Cleansing, healing, protection, purification

Valerian (*Valeriana officinalis*): Baneful magic, banishing, fear, hex and curse breaking, nightmares, protection, reflecting evil, removal, slowing down, stopping behaviors

Watercress (*Nasturtium officinale*): Dragon power, dragon spirits

White Pepper (*Piper nigrum*): Banishment, fire, healing, heat, power, protection, removal

Wintergreen (*Gaultheria procumbens*): Cooling off, healing, hex breaking, protection

Wood Betony (*Pedicularis canadensis*): Cleansing, hex breaking, protection, purification

Woodruff (*Galium odoratum*): Control of the situation, courage, power, prosperity, protection, strength, success, victory

Wormwood (*Artemisia absinthium*): Altered states of consciousness, astral travel, divination, mental powers, psychic senses, psychic sight, psychic work, spiritual development, spirituality, trance work

Yarrow (*Achillea millefolium*): Attracting customers, attracting love, drawing money, healing, hex breaking, removal

Yellow Dock (*Rumex crispus*): Attracting love, attracting sales, money, prosperity, success

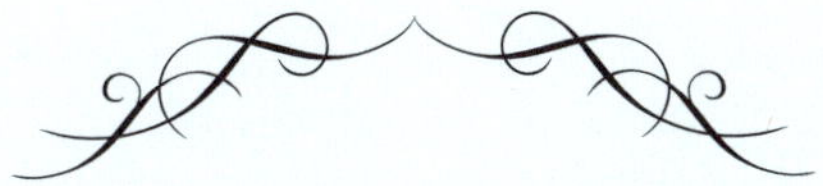

Crystal, Stone & Mineral Correspondences

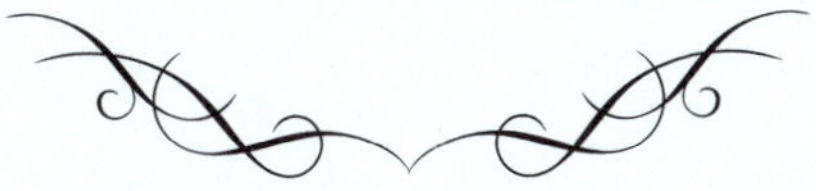

While crystals and minerals are not used in the creation of magical powders, magical powders can be used to bless or empower these curios.

Amethyst: Healing, mental focus, psychic development, psychic powers, psychic work

Aventurine: Money, prosperity, success

Blue Calcite: Healing

Carnelian: Desire, love, passion, romance, sex

Fluorite: Meditation, mental clarity, psychic senses

Fool's Gold (Iron Pyrite): Money, prosperity, success

Goldstone: Attracting customers, money, sales, success

Jasper: Protection

Lapis Lazuli: Communication, understanding

Lodestone: Good luck

Obsidian: Protection

Onyx: Protection

Saltpeter: Banishment, changing luck, cleansing, hex and jinx breaking, luck, removal

Sea Salt: Absorption of energy, cleansing, neutralization, neutralizing negativity, protection, removal

Sodalite: Communication, understanding

Sulphur: Jinxing, justice, reversal

Quartz:

Citrine: Luck, money, prosperity, substitute for goldstone, success, wealth

Clear: Healing, luck, magic, peace, power, powering up other materials

Rose: Family, love, peace

Smoky: Protection, neutralization of negative energy, reversal

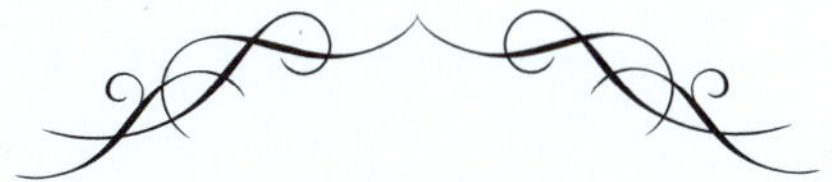

Dirt Correspondences

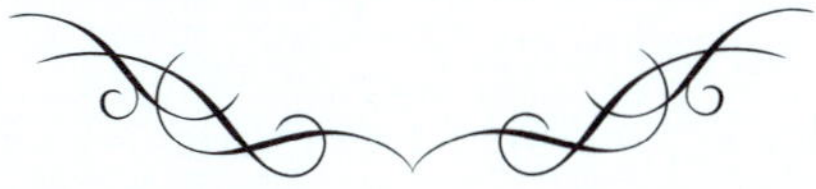

The earliest form of magical powder was that of dirt. Today, dirt is still a powerful magical tool. Many spells, formulas, and workings use dirt gathered from specific locations. The following is just a small sample of the types of dirt that can be found and worked with. For more information on the magic of dirt, read my book *Divine Dirt*.

Animal Tracks: Contains the power of the animal that laid the tracks

Ant Hill: Removes blocks to financial stability, removes blocks to money

Bank/Credit Union/Financial Institution: Financial stability, financial success, money, protection of money, success

Bar/Nightclub: People, socialization

Courthouse: Dealing with legal issues, justice

Crossroads: Magic, power, sending energy out to all directions of the universe, wishes

Graveyard/Cemetery: Ancestor work, baneful magic, death, destruction

Home: Represents the home and everyone in it, used as a household personal effect

Library/School/Training Center: Opening up opportunities

Mall: Customers, money, sales

Shipping Center/Transportation Center: Motion, moving away, moving to

Stop Sign: Ending behaviors, stopping

Swamp: Change, chaos, confusion

Tidal: Change, chaos, confusion

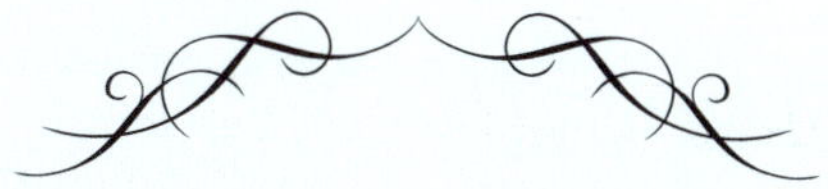

Manufactured Curio Correspondences

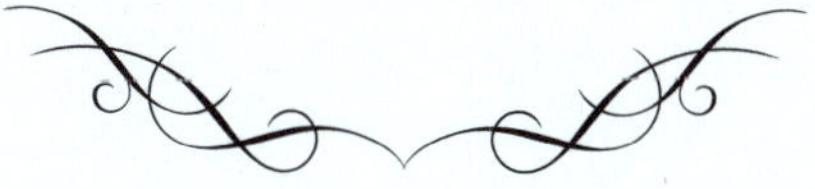

When you cast a spell, you do not need to focus on just materials from the natural world. Materials that have been created by humans, or manufactured curios, have their own place and space in magical work.

Aluminum Foil: Reflection, reversal, protection

Anvil Dust: Protection

Ash: Absorption, neutralization

Baby Powder: Attraction, beauty, healing, love; it is a neutrally charged base powder

Brooms: Banishment, cleansing, protection, removal; they can be used to disperse floor sweeps

Cash (Toy and Real): Money

Cat Litter (Fresh): Absorption, feline energy, neutralization

Cat Litter (Used): Baneful magic, hexing

Charcoal: Neutralization, protection

Crystal Skulls: Ancestors

Gunpowder: Baneful magic, death, destruction, hexing

Hand Fan: Dispersal of incense and powders, wafting incense

Heart-Shaped Crystals: Healing, love, self-love

Horseshoe: Horse energy, luck, success

Magnet: Attracting good luck, repelling bad luck

Magnetic Sand: Attraction, money, pulling away from you, pulling toward you, reflection, repelling

Mirrors: Reflection, reversal

Nail: Baneful magic, protection

Needles: Baneful magic, protection

Pins: Baneful magic, protection

Red Brick Dust: Protection

Scissors: Clearing, cutting, removal

Skeleton Key: Block breaking, opening doors, opportunities

Incense Recipes

Many people enjoy using incense as a part of their spell and ritual work. Several spells in this text use incense as a tool. Here are some incense formulas you can use in your magical workings.

Lucky Incense

Luck is one type of blessing that spirits and the universe can bestow upon us. Use this incense to bring the blessing of luck into your life.

MATERIALS

- ¼ cup (60 ml) grains of paradise (*Aframomum melegueta*) (for luck, success, prosperity, to attract good luck)
- ½ tablespoon (7 ml) clover (*Trifolium repens*) (for good luck)

- ½ tablespoon (7 ml) peony flowers (*Paeonia officinalis*) (for good luck, blessings of luck, to attract luck)
- 1 teaspoon (5 ml) saltpeter (to change luck)

Generic Ritual Blessings Incense

This incense is based on one of the first ritual incense blends I ever crafted. This is a good all-purpose incense. It can be used for protection, cleansing, blessing, and psychic or spiritual work.

MATERIALS

- ½ cup (125 ml) mugwort (*Artemisia vulgaris*) (for blessing, cleansing, power of magic and witchcraft)
- ½ tablespoon (7 ml) angelica root (*Angelica archangelica*) (for blessing, cleansing, protection)
- ½ tablespoon (7 ml) basil (*Ocimum basilicum*) (for blessing, cleansing)
- ½ tablespoon (7 ml) frankincense (*Boswellia sacra*) (for blessing, cleansing, to make sacred)
- ½ tablespoon (7 ml) sage (*Salvia officinalis*) (for blessing, cleansing, protection)

General Money Incense

This is an incense for general money work. Use in any non–fast cash money works. Use a fast cash incense when you need money quickly.

MATERIALS

- ¾ cup (180 ml) pine needles (*Pinus* spp.) (for fertility, money, success)
- 1½ tablespoon (22 ml) alfalfa (*Medicago sativa*) (for fast cash, fertility, money, success)
- ½ tablespoon (7 ml) marigold flowers (*Calendula officinalis*) (for fertility, money, success)
- ½ tablespoon (7 ml) cinnamon (*Cinnamomum verum*) (for fertility, money, success)
- ½ tablespoon (7 ml) fenugreek (*Trigonella foenum-graecum*) (for fertility, money, success)

Dragon Fire Protection Incense

One of the types of spirits I work with a lot in my practice is that of dragons. Dragon spirits are powerful and will protect their allies as best they can. Evil spells and attacks often fail when confronted with dragon fire protection.

MATERIALS

- 1 cup (250 ml) basil (*Ocimum basilicum*) (for connection to spirits, dragons, protection)
- 2½ tablespoons (37 ml) dragon's blood resin (*Dracaena cinnabari*) (for dragons, power, protection, strength)
- ½ tablespoon (7 ml) cayenne pepper (*Capsicum annuum*) (for fire, protection, to repel evil)
- ½ tablespoon (7 ml) rosemary (*Salvia rosmarinus*) (for dragon power, protection, removal, spirit energy, to attract spirits, cut and clear)

- ½ tablespoon (7 ml) watercress (*Nasturtium officinale*) (for dragons, dragon power, dragon spirit, protection)

Sweet Healing Incense

This is a healing incense that smells sweet. Its aroma allows you to relax and be at peace, enabling your body and mind to heal. Use this incense to provide a soothing boost to any healing work.

MATERIALS

- ¾ cup (180 ml) goldenseal (*Hydrastis canadensis*) (for healing)
- 1 tablespoon (15 ml) allspice (*Pimenta dioica*) (for healing)
- 1 tablespoon (15 ml) angelica (*Angelica archangelica*) (for healing)
- ½ tablespoon (7 ml) chamomile (*Matricaria recutita*) (for healing, peace, relaxation)
- ½ tablespoon (7 ml) lavender (*Lavandula officinalis*) (for healing, peace, relaxation)

House Cleanse & Bless Incense

This incense is great for cleansing and blessing your home. Ideally you would perform the cleansing and blessing shortly before you move in. Once moved in, this incense works well to keep the house cleansed, making it a place where everyone feels safe, happy, and protected.

MATERIALS

- ¾ cup (180 ml) basil (*Ocimum basilicum*) (for blessing, cleansing)
- 1 tablespoon (15 ml) frankincense (*Boswellia sacra*) (for consecration)
- 1 tablespoon (15 ml) sage (*Salvia officinalis*) (for protection against the evil eye, to cleanse)
- ½ tablespoon (7 ml) cedar (*Cedrus libani*) (for cleansing)
- ½ tablespoon (7 ml) lemon balm (*Melissa officinalis*) (for blessing, cleansing)

Sweet Love Incense

The sweet scent of this incense works to attract a gentle and romantic love to you.

MATERIALS

- ¾ cup (180 ml) red rose petals (*Rosa rubiginosa*) (for love, romance)
- 1 tablespoon (15 ml) passionflower (*Passiflora incarnata*) (for desire, love, romance)
- ½ tablespoon (7 ml) catnip (*Nepeta cataria*) (for happiness, joy, love, romance)
- ½ tablespoon (7 ml) lavender (*Lavandula officinalis*) (for desire, happiness, joy, love, peace)
- ½ tablespoon (7 ml) lemon verbena (*Lippia citriodora*) (for desire, love, romance)
- ½ tablespoon (7 ml) patchouli (*Pogostemon cablin*) (for desire, love)

Psychic Eyes Incense

Use this incense blend to enhance your psychic sight. Images, senses, and feelings will be clearer, crisp, and easier to understand. Combine it with any other mental powers or psychic/divination incense to boost its effect.

MATERIALS

- ½ cup (125 ml) eyebright (*Euphrasia rostkoviana*) (for mental focus, psychic power, psychic senses, psychic sight)
- ½ tablespoon (7 ml) anise seeds (*Illicium verum*) (for divination, mental powers, psychic senses, psychic sight)
- ½ tablespoon (7 ml) ginkgo leaves (*Ginkgo biloba*) (for mental clarity, mental powers, psychic abilities)
- ½ tablespoon (7 ml) rosemary (*Salvia rosmarinus*) (for memory, mental focus, mental powers, psychic senses)
- ½ tablespoon (7 ml) wormwood (*Artemisia absinthium*) (for divination, mental powers, psychic senses, psychic sight)

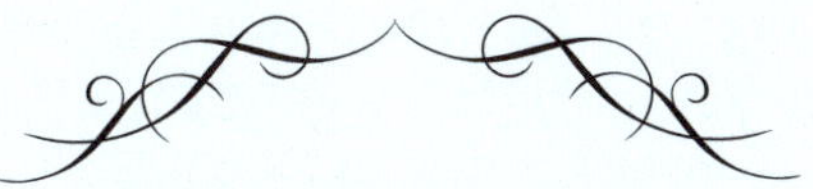

Conclusion

Magic can seem overwhelming and confusing at first. From the different types of energy that can be worked with to the mental focus needed to control it, there is a lot of work that goes into the practice of working spells and magic. It is true that learning the skills to work magic takes time and effort, but if anyone wants to be good at something, they need to put in the work to develop the skills. Once that foundation is laid, using the skills seems effortless.

Finding the time to work magic can be very discouraging given the world that we live in. Most of our days are packed with work and appointments. It can be hard to find the time to engage in magical and spiritual activities. The social expectations of engaging in current pop culture over personal growth can make it difficult to choose magic over watching movies, playing video games, and socializing.

The best way to develop these skills and make magic a part of your life is by engaging in simple daily practices. This is where using charged oils, incenses, and magical powders comes into play. Once these materials have been crafted, they contain a magical charge that just needs to be released.

Throughout this text, you have learned skills that will allow you to work spells almost in an instant. From awakening spirits to working with vibrational energy, the skills learned through this book will not only empower your magic but allow you to access magic whenever you want.

The powders created allow you to work magic simply by sprinkling them and focusing on your intent. Through learning the skills and formulas within this text, you have found that magic can be utilized as part of your day-to-day life. Working with magical powders provides a way for you to use magic right away or store it for another day.

Remember that magic doesn't have to be fancy. It can be as simple as sprinkling some powder in your shoes and walking to manifest your desire. Magic can also take the form of the foods we eat and the scents we use to make the home feel more welcoming. Love, money, peace, protection—anything you desire—can be manifested through the use of magical powders.

The more we use our magical skills, the more effective our magic becomes. By using magic daily, our lives can truly be the ones that we want to have. Don't wait to use a spell or work until there is great need. Use magic on a regular basis so that the difficulties, problems, and issues in your life are minimal. Reclaim your magical power and take control of your life.

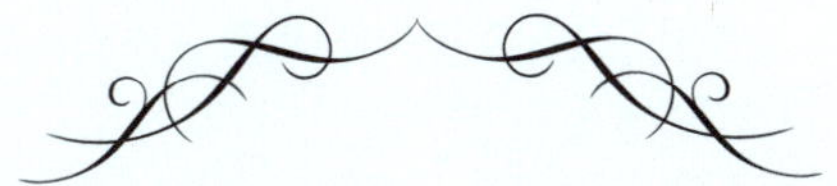

Acknowledgments

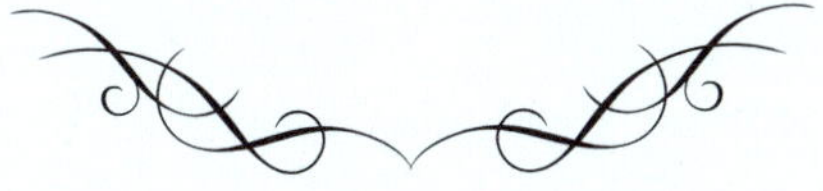

First off, I would like to acknowledge and thank Gale Gladstorm for taking over as my agent after her husband passed. It means a lot to me that she continues to believe in me and the work that I do, encouraging me to submit all the ideas that I have.

Second, I want to thank and acknowledge Heather Greene and the rest of the staff at Llewellyn Publishing. Writing for them is a dream come true. With the help of the editors, I have been able to grow as a writer and improve my skills substantially. The encouragement I have received to keep up the work helps keep my passion for writing alive.

Finally, I want to thank my husband and partner, Ben. From the beginning, he has always believed in my ability to make my dreams come true. He supported me in opening Mystic Echoes and has continued to support me as I work as a writer. His presence keeps me grounded while letting me reach for the stars as I dream.

APPENDIX I

Recipes & Spells in Order of Appearance

Part I: Magical Powder Basics

Witches' Salts

Sweetening Magical Powders

Floor Sweeps

Part III: Resources

Incense Recipes

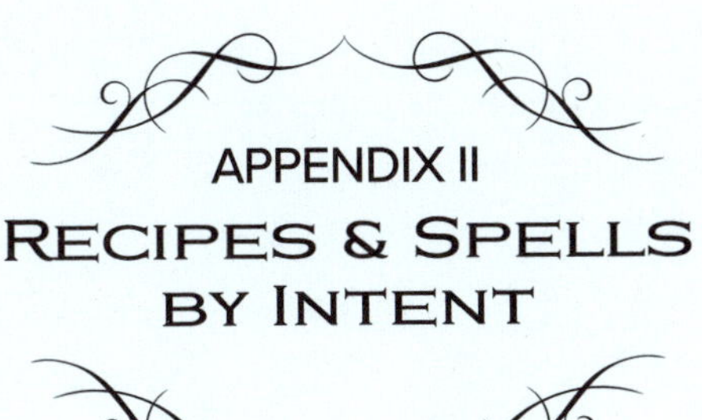

APPENDIX II
Recipes & Spells by Intent

Baneful Magic

Banishment

Cleansing

Controlling

Customer Sales & Services

Divination

Employment

Fast Cash

Fertility

Friends & Friendship

Healing

Hex Breaking

House & Home

Justice

Legal Matters

Luck

Lust

Meditation

Mental Health

Money

Prosperity & Success

Protection

Psychic Development

Relationships

Rituals

Spirit Work

Sweetening

Wishes

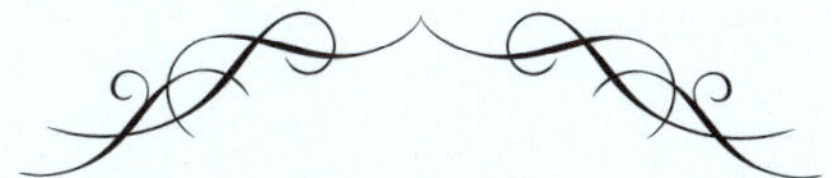

Recommended Reading

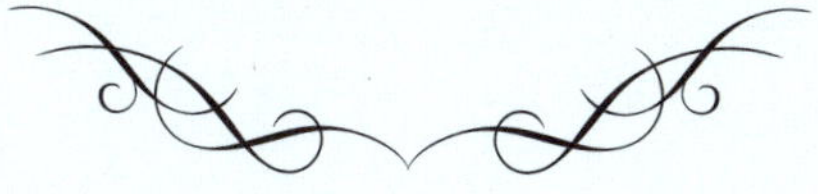

Backwoods Shamanism: An Introduction to the Old-Time American Folk Magic of Hoodoo Conjure and Rootwork by Ray "Doctor Hawk" Hess

Backwoods Witchcraft: Conjure & Folk Magic from Appalachia by Jake Richards

Basic Magick: A Practical Guide by Phillip Cooper

The Big Book of Practical Spells: Everyday Magic That Works by Judika Illes

The Big Little Book of Magick: A Wiccan's Guide to Altars, Candles, Pendulums, and Healing Spells by D. J. Conway

Blackthorn's Botanical Magic: The Green Witch's Guide to Essential Oils for Spellcraft, Ritual, and Healing by Amy Blackthorn

The Book of English Magic by Philip Carr-Gomm and Richard Heygate

The Candle and the Crossroads: A Book of Appalachian Conjure and Southern Root Work by Orion Foxwood

The Casting of Spells: Creating a Magickal Life through the Words of True Will by Christopher Penczak

A Compendium of Herbal Magick by Paul Beyerl

The Complete Book of Incense, Oils & Brews by Scott Cunningham

The Conjure Workbook Volume 1: Working the Root by Starr Casas

Crossroads of Conjure: The Roots and Practices of Granny Magic, Hoodoo, Brujería, and Curanderismo by Katrina Rasbold

Cunningham's Encyclopedia of Crystal, Gem & Metal Magic by Scott Cunningham

Cunningham's Encyclopedia of Magical Herbs by Scott Cunningham

Cunningham's Encyclopedia of Wicca in the Kitchen by Scott Cunningham

Cunningham's Magical Sampler: Collected Writings and Spells from the Renowned Wiccan Author by Scott Cunningham

Earth, Air, Fire & Water: More Techniques of Natural Magic by Scott Cunningham

Earth Power: Techniques of Natural Magic by Scott Cunningham

The Encyclopedia of 5,000 Spells: The Ultimate Reference Book for the Magical Arts by Judika Illes

Everyday Magic: Spells & Rituals for Modern Living by Dorothy Morrison

The Flame in the Cauldron: A Book of Old-Style Witchery by Orion Foxwood

Folk Witchcraft: A Guide to Lore, Land, and the Familiar Spirit for the Solitary Practitioner by Roger J. Horne

A Grimoire for Modern Cunningfolk by Peter Paddon

Hoodoo Bible Magic: Sacred Secrets of Scriptural Sorcery by Miss Michaele and Professor Charles Porterfield

The Hoodoo Bible: The 7-in-1 Root Doctor's Companion to Black Folk Magic: Herb and Rootwork, Conjure Oils and Mojo Bags, Easy and Advanced Spells, Candle Magic and Divination to Get Your Mojo Workin' by Mama Marie

Hoodoo Herbal by Starr Casas

Hoodoo Herb and Root Magic: A Materia Magica of African-American Conjure by Catherine Yronwode

Hoodoo Your Love: Conjure the Love You Want (and Keep It) by Starr Casas

The Inner Temple of Witchcraft: Magick, Meditation, and Psychic Development by Christoper Penczak

Instant Magick: Ancient Wisdom, Modern Spellcraft by Christopher Penczak

Introduction to Southern Conjure (DVD) by Orion Foxwood

The Kybalion by Three Initiates

The Little Book of Curses and Maledictions for Everyday Use by Dawn Rae Downton

Living Conjure: The Practice of Southern Folk Magic by Starr Casas

Magical Herbalism: The Secret Craft of the Wise by Scott Cunningham

The Magical Power of the Saints: Evocations & Candle Rituals by Ray T. Malbrough

Magick in Theory and Practice by Aleister Crowley

Magic's in the Bag: Creating Spellbinding Gris Gris Bags & Sachets by Jude Bradley and Cher'e Dastugue Coen

Magic When You Need It: 150 Spells You Can't Live Without by Judika Illes

The Master Book of Herbalism by Paul Beyerl

Old Style Conjure: Hoodoo, Rootwork & Folk Magic by Starr Casas

Papa Jim's Herbal Magic Workbook: How to Use Herbs for Magical Purposes, an A–Z Guide by Papa Jim

Powers of the Psalms by Anna Riva

Practical Magic for Beginners: Techniques & Rituals to Focus Magical Energy by Brandy Williams

Practical Solitary Magic by Nancy B. Watson

Rootwork: Using the Folk Magick of Black America for Love, Money, and Success by Tayannah Lee McQuillar

The Secret Keys of Conjure: Unlocking the Mysteries of American Folk Magic by Chas Bogan

Southern Cunning: Folkloric Witchcraft in the American South by Aaron Oberon

Spells and How They Work by Janet Farrar and Stewart Farrar

True Magick: A Beginner's Guide by Amber K

Utterly Wicked: Hexes, Curses, and Other Unsavory Notions by Dorothy Morrison

The Witch and Wizard Training Guide by Sirona Knight

The Witch's Bag of Tricks: Personalize Your Magick & Kickstart Your Craft by Melanie Marquis

A Witch's World of Magick: Expanding Your Practice with Techniques & Traditions from Diverse Cultures by Melanie Marquis

Working Conjure: A Guide to Hoodoo Folk Magic by Hoodoo Sen Moise

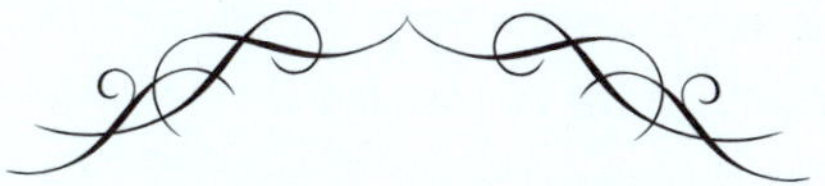

Works Cited

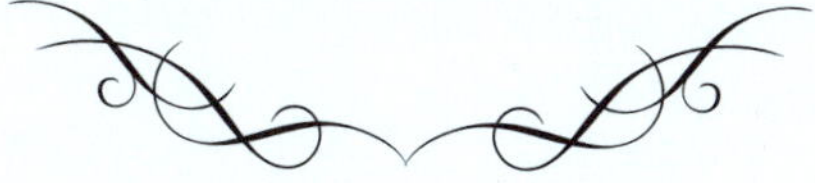

Exodus 12:22–23 (New International Version). BibleGateway. Accessed September 3, 2024. https://www.biblegateway.com/passage/?search=Exodus%2012%3A22-23&version=NIV.

Illes, Judika. *The Encyclopedia of 5,000 Spells: The Ultimate Reference Book for the Magical Arts*. HarperOne, 2008.

Matthew 13:31–32 (New International Version). BibleGateway. Accessed July 2, 2025. https://www.biblegateway.com/passage/?search=Matthew%2013%3A31-32&version=NIV.

1 Corinthians 13:4–7 (New International Version). BibleGateway. Accessed December 26, 2024. https://www.biblegateway.com/passage/?search=1%20Corinthians%2013%3A4-7&version=NIV.

"Prayer to St. Michael the Archangel." St. Michael the Archangel Roman Catholic Church. Accessed June 14, 2024. https://saintmichaelcc.org/prayer-to-st-michael-the-archangel.

Psalm 23 (New International Version). BibleGateway. Accessed September 9, 2024. https://www.biblegateway.com/passage/?search=Psalm%2023&version=NIV.

Psalm 31:4–8 (New International Version). BibleGateway. Accessed October 22, 2024. https://www.biblegateway.com/passage/?search=Psalm%2031%3A4-8&version=NIV.

Psalm 90:17 (New International Version). BibleGateway. Accessed July 17, 2024. https://www.biblegateway.com/passage/?search=Psalm%2090%3A17&version=NIV.

Psalm 103:1–5 (New International Version). BibleGateway. Accessed September 3, 2024. https://www.biblegateway.com/passage/?search=Psalm%20103%3A1-5&version=NIV.

Psalm 140:1–11 (New International Version). BibleGateway. Accessed August 1, 2024. https://www.biblegateway.com/passage/?search=Psalm%20140%3A1-11&version=NIV.